Grow
your wealth
faster with
alternative assets

Grow your wealth *faster* with

A Complete Guide to the New Universe of Investment Opportunities

alternative assets

Travis Miller

WILEY

First published in 2023 by John Wiley & Sons Australia, Ltd
Level 4, 600 Bourke St, Melbourne Victoria 3000, Australia.

Typeset in Warnock Pro 12pt/16pt

© JettGusBuddy Pty Ltd 2023

The moral rights of the author have been asserted

ISBN: 978-1-394-18499-6

 A catalogue record for this book is available from the National Library of Australia

Cover design by Wiley
Cover image: © Tackey/Shutterstock

Figure 6.2: Toy truck: © Denis Kovin/Shutterstock
Figure 6.1: Aerial view of cars: © Avigator Fortuner/Shutterstock

Disclaimer
The material in this publication is of the nature of general comment only, and does not represent professional advice. It is not intended to provide specific guidance for particular circumstances and it should not be relied on as the basis for any decision to take action or not take action on any matter which it covers. Readers should obtain professional advice where appropriate, before making any such decision. To the maximum extent permitted by law, the author and publisher disclaim all responsibility and liability to any person, arising directly or indirectly from any person taking or not taking action based on the information in this publication.

Contents

Introduction

Alternative assets are an exciting new investment opportunity for individual investors. Well, strictly speaking they are not new, but until recently they have only been available to the big players, such as institutions and incredibly wealthy families, who can invest anywhere from $5 million to $50 million in one trade. But thanks to some outside-the-box thinking combined with innovations in technology, things are shifting and now individual investors like you and me can pool our investing power and get on board.

What makes alternatives so attractive is their risk-return profile. They can provide more favourable returns for the amount of risk than traditional investments. As non-traditional asset classes, they can get a bit complex, but there is a premium to be earned from complexity, and they are also very interesting, so it's fun to get your head around them.

So what is an alternative asset? The best way to think about alternative assets is in terms of what they are not. They are not listed equities (shares), over-the-counter fixed income or cash, term deposits, cash management trusts or traditional managed funds. These are all traditional assets available in the public market. Alternative assets are everything else. They often take the form of capital provided to private companies in various debt or credit structures (which is where they get really interesting). They can also be things like commercial property, infrastructure, agriculture and commodities.

A key difference with alternative assets is that they are illiquid, which means that you put your money down for a fixed amount of time — say 18 months — and you can't get access to it during that time. A liquid investment is one where you can get your money back (or what's left of it) whenever you like. If you buy shares today, you could sell them tomorrow. With illiquid investments, you can't get your money out whenever you choose, but because of this, you typically earn a greater return. So, with alternative assets you're not necessarily taking on more loss risk, but you get paid more because you've committed to a fixed or unknown term of investment, which is a scarcer form of capital. Hence, through a simple supply-and-demand dynamic, you can earn more!

There's a further supply-and-demand piece in play, which is the fact that alternative assets are not an off-the-shelf product. They are hard to find and complex to package, so traditional financial planners and private wealth companies don't usually offer them broadly. Most wealth firms are built for scale, so they typically try to offer low-touch, low-service, commoditised models such as managed accounts and discretionary portfolios. Alternative assets often don't fit into such models because they aren't commoditised, meaning no two alternative assets are exactly the same. This is another reason why they typically have greater returns for similar or lower risk: fewer investors means less capital available to these investment opportunities.

Less supply of capital (from investors) + more demand (from capital raisers) = greater returns (but for the same or less risk).

The percentage of alternative assets that people generally have in their portfolios is currently quite low, perhaps around 5 per cent. To really make your money work for you, I suggest allocating approximately 20 to 30 per cent in alternatives as a good starting point.

The majority of my investments are in alternative assets. I have been investing for a long time, but I only really threw myself into alternatives in 2008 when I was working for Deutsche Bank and realised there were some pretty cool opportunities in this asset class. At the time there were a lot of barriers to access. Historically, alternative assets have been difficult to find. Even if you find them, you then have to put in place very complex legal documentation. Because I worked in an investment bank, I understood where to look and how things worked. If I'd been an average investor, I would have struggled to get access to these investments (or even know they existed). This is because traditionally, alternative asset opportunities are promoted to banks, large institutional investors and large family offices, not individuals like you or me. This lack of access was the key — and frustrating — barrier that drove co-founder Rob Nankivell and me to start iPartners, which was the first alternative assets investment platform of its kind.

Investment platforms such as iPartners have totally changed the landscape for direct investors to gain access to alternative assets. Investors can now educate themselves, search, research and access investments in smaller denominations than they could in the past. Technology has enabled this by making the aggregation of investor capital efficient and scalable. Investors can put in as little as $10 000 per trade. After they invest, they can review their investments by logging onto the platform to see how their investment is performing. The most exciting feature is the ability to potentially access secondary liquidity on what has historically been an illiquid asset, which is a fancy way of saying if you need to sell your alternative assets before the fixed term is up, the iPartners platform may be able to find someone who will buy them from you. This is a bonus because, remember, the good risk-return profile of alternatives is due in part to the fact that they are illiquid assets.

A wide range of investors use our platform: from financial professionals who work in alternative assets and want access to similar opportunities for their personal investing, to doctors, lawyers, tradespeople and business owners who want to diversify their portfolio with alternative opportunities. To invest in the majority of alternative assess (under current regulations) you must be a wholesale investor and hold net assets worth more than $2.5 million, or your gross annual personal income must be at least $250 000 for the last two years — this can include income from a business if you're a small business owner.

I'm passionate about alternative assets. They can open up an entire new universe of investment opportunities for the individual investor. So I wrote this book to share the dream!

Part I of the book looks at the history of alternative assets (you can skip that bit if it's not your thing), how to invest in them, things to look out for, and how trades are found and executed. In part II I run through all the alternative asset classes and explain them as simply as I can to give you a broad understanding of the range of opportunities in this growing space.

If you have any questions or you just want to chat with me, please email me at alternatives@ipartners.com.au.

Travis

The what, why and how of alternative assets

Where it all started

Let's start out by taking a look at the recent history of alternative assets and how I got into them.

I can't talk about the history of alternative assets without framing it around the GFC (global financial crisis), which was an investment game changer. So here's a quick refresher before we get into it. As you may well know, the GFC was a severe worldwide economic crisis that occurred from mid 2007 to early 2009. It was the most serious financial crisis since the Great Depression of the 1930s. It was caused by house prices in the United States falling and a rising number of US borrowers being unable to repay their mortgages. As a result, various US banks held trillions of dollars of worthless loans. Because of the linkages in the global financial system, this downturn in the United States spread to the rest of the world, resulting in a deep global recession. Millions of people lost their jobs, and banks incurred large losses and ended up having to rely on government money to avoid bankruptcy.

Before the GFC, alternative asset opportunities for everyday investors in Australia mainly came out of banks as what's known in the business as 'structured products'. The underlying assets tended to be hedge funds, alternative funds or products combining a deposit with embedded derivatives (a derivative is a contract between at least two parties that derives its value from something else, such as an underlying asset or event outcome). These products were called 'structured' because they tended to have a loan embedded in them, or some other complexity. (We'll dive into structured products in part 2). The aim of the banks in making these products available was to effectively build their loan books by lending money to retail and wholesale investors so they could gain access to these assets. The banks, in turn, collected both interest on the loan and product fees.

Post GFC, a large proportion of these assets underperformed, and it wasn't a great experience for investors because of the loan element. When the market turned down, investors had limited prospects of positive returns from the underlying assets, but were locked into contracts that required them to continue paying interest. Investors lost money and banks suffered reputational damage. No-one was happy. Since then, we haven't really seen banks issue leveraged alternative asset products in Australia.

In the early 2000s property trusts and real property asset investing started to emerge: some listed, some unlisted. The listed property trusts were called REITs (Real Estate Investment Trusts) or diversified property exposures. The unlisted versions were private. For example, five investors would put in $1 million each and then buy the equity in a small shopping centre in, say, Newcastle for $5 million. Property debt specifically became very popular — and still is. Property debt typically involves a private lender, lending to a developer.

Property is one of the key alternative assets that investors invest in today.

Property debt is such a popular alternative asset that it's become quite mainstream — to the point where I believe it almost shouldn't be classed as an alternative asset anymore.

Since the mid 2010s we've seen the emergence of crowdfunders in the alternatives space. These are entities that aggregate very small amounts of capital to provide angel and seed funding to start-up businesses. These crowdfunding platforms don't necessarily have high-quality, vetted deal flow though, or much investment success of note. They're simply a location where investors can put small amounts into early-stage companies, which all investors know is a highly risky investment to make. There's no reliable promise of returns nor is much obvious due diligence done. Regardless of the quality of investments, they have become an access point for investors looking to gain exposure to (that is, to have the opportunity to invest in) venture capital and private, equity like investments.

My venture into alternative assets

When the GFC hit, I was a director at Deutsche Bank Australia. I got to witness changes in the investment banking world from the inside during this volatile time. I was lucky to see opportunities emerge for investing personally during a time that was difficult for so many. These opportunities were in alternative assets, and they were unbelievable. Because virtually all markets were crashing, anyone who wanted to buy could pretty much buy at literally any price. I had some money at the time, so I was lucky that I could be a buyer when most people were selling. These investment opportunities were only available for those with cash, a contrarian view on markets and courage to take risk, which means I started my journey into alternative assets at a time when the ride was pretty wild!

I'd been working in banking for about seven years, although it wasn't my original career of choice. When I was at high school, sport was my main thing and studies were an afterthought at best. My final HSC grades were pretty woeful, but it didn't matter to me at the time because I was drafted to play AFL straight out of high school and spent 1992 at the Fitzroy Football Club (now merged into Brisbane Lions) and part of 1993 at Melbourne and Collingwood football clubs, so for a while I was living the dream.

But the dream didn't last. I rode on talent rather than putting in the effort to really do well — even in sport, which I enjoyed. I look back at my younger self and think my head just wasn't quite screwed on yet! I had some growing up to do.

After finishing up with the AFL I drifted around the personal training and gym industry for a while, and gradually woke up to the importance of education. All my mates had already got their degrees and were kicking off their careers while I was still working part-time jobs in gyms and pools. So I enrolled in a Bachelor of Arts in Recreation and Fitness. For the first time, I realised I was reasonably intelligent and I enjoyed studying.

By this time I was managing a gym and running my own personal training business on the side. I realised I had some business smarts, which eventually gave me the idea that I could go into business myself. So after completing my Bachelor of Arts, I went straight into doing a Master of Business Finance at Victoria University.

When I started studying finance I thought, 'Actually, this is pretty cool.' It was challenging. I needed to think and solve problems, do modelling and regression analyses — things that were really interesting and different. That's when it became fun for me. I'd bumbled through my BA, but I really applied myself when I got into finance.

I completed my Master of Finance at around 24, then started out as a junior e-commerce analyst at the ANZ, helping them build an online capital markets platform, which was well ahead of our times in the early 2000s. (A sign of things to come?) During that first year at ANZ I did a Master of Business Administration (MBA) at Victoria University on the side.

I got lots of great opportunities at ANZ. Throughout my whole career I've had great bosses who were willing to trust and stretch me, for which I'm very grateful. By 2003 I'd got my Chartered Financial Analyst (CFA), which is one of the top qualifications in the industry, and had a new position as Associate Director of Credit Derivatives. I was sitting in the dealing room doing a lot of structured credit and credit analysis, which was really cool. It was pre GFC, the markets were absolutely flying and I was sitting in the hottest area. Banking was an awesome place to work, with lots of problem solving and lots of different trades. I was learning a lot. There were jobs everywhere and people were getting paid really well, so it was a fun time to be involved.

I was doing well in my job and started getting approached by other investment banks about working for them. In 2006 I accepted an offer for a director role at Deutsche Bank.

The work involved a lot of problem solving, complex modelling and analysis. There were all these inputs or tools to put together to create a product that was investable. It needed to be packaged nicely so that institutions could simply come along and buy it without needing to solve the problem themselves.

> ### *I loved the complexity of putting these products together and the simplicity for the investor once I'd packaged them.*

This has been the basis of my work ever since: presenting complex investment opportunities to investors in an understandable form.

Around this time I also did the Financial Risk Manager (FRM®) program, which is an international accreditation with a six-hour exam. I completed this exam primarily for general interest and continued learning, although in hindsight it was very relevant because possibly the most dominant afterthought of the GFC was risk management. Risk management was, and still is, one of the hot topics in the post-mortem of the GFC.

The GFC was primarily a liquidity and credit crisis, so fewer liquid assets — and those exposed to credit, such as alternative assets — were impacted. Everything basically became illiquid, meaning if you owned an asset you couldn't get out (a lesson to be discussed later: liquidity can be your friend or enemy depending on your investment horizons).

Even though the sector was distressed, the GFC created a whole pile of opportunities for investors and for me personally. Credit derivatives lost their popularity, but people and institutions were still looking for investment opportunities and there were a lot of investors with cash to deploy. We helped investors find distressed credit opportunities that had a reasonable chance of rebounding and performing. I also began looking into different asset classes that were starting to become more popular, such as real assets and equity derivatives. So the GFC helped me diversify my knowledge and look at different investment options. It was a unique opportunity to learn something new. I moved with the times and pivoted to what was the next opportunity post GFC. I became that guy who had lived through a crisis and come out the other side intact, with lessons learned!

In 2011, I moved from Deutsche Bank to work for UBS Investment Bank as an executive director. I headed up alternative asset distribution across all asset classes in the markets business. My role was to look across all asset classes and identify any opportunity to solve a problem or tailor an assets risk profile, then implement and execute those trades with the investor base. It was a solutions-based role that needed out-of-the-box thinking. We put together trades across equities, rates, fixed income — all sorts of things. I did that for six years, finishing as a managing director — which is the top corporate title at the bank — and I loved it!

Every time I've moved jobs it's been because I felt like I'd learned all I could in the area where I was working, and I wanted the next challenge. I love opportunities to learn about a new product, run a new business or grow something. By 2016 my work at UBS had become very commoditised, and a bit boring, because there was less problem solving involved. The long-term response to the GFC meant that banks were doing less interesting alternative asset deals. These changes were happening across the whole banking sector at the time.

Banks lost interest in opportunities that required problem solving because they were seen as riskier. They just wanted to do more of the same, simple, repeatable trades. I think it was what the regulator wanted them to do (which was achieved to a degree), but was also a lot less exciting for employees who enjoyed solving complex problems. Once banking moved in that direction they lost a lot of good people.

By this time I had completed my Masters of Business Law at Sydney University. (Yes, I had still been studying this whole time, very part-time though!) It was difficult, but I loved all the tax subjects. That might sound strange, but with everything you do in financial products, you have to consider the tax outcome for the investor. There are different legal structures and different ways of delivering an investment product, which means you need to have a good knowledge of the taxation of unit trusts, bare trusts, other trusts, companies, SMSFs (self-managed super funds) and tax as an individual. You also need to understand the various legal forms of assets exposures, such as debt, equity, hybrid, deferred purchase agreements, contracts and onshore or offshore instruments. To make sure you deliver the investor the best opportunity to have a good outcome from their investment you need to have a thorough knowledge in this, which is why I enjoyed it so much. Tax might sound dry, but when you apply that knowledge to improve investment outcomes, it's very interesting.

So with my Masters of Business Law and a Level 2 CAIA (Chartered Alternative Investment Analyst, another global accreditation) completed and my job no longer satisfying me intellectually, it was time to think of the next opportunity. An ex-client of mine and I had been discussing an interesting idea for a couple of years — it was time to make a move.

Enter iPartners

That ex-client was Rob Nankivell. We'd been talking about potential opportunities in the marketplace and had come to share the view that the biggest opportunity was in alternative assets. We were seeing great trades that we wanted to invest in ourselves, but the barriers to doing so (access and not enough capital) meant we couldn't. But what if we started a business that solved these barriers and made it possible for individual investors to invest in alternatives?

Rob and I started having regular meetings, along with Norm King (a tech guy) and Chris Reade (a structurer guy who turned up not long after) to discuss how we could put this business in place. We knew the average investor struggled to get access to alternative assets, but thanks to our careers in the institutional world, Rob and I knew what the alternative asset opportunities were and how to find them, so we could be the bridge.

But there was one problem: these opportunities required much larger sums than an average investor has — often anywhere from $5 million to $100 million. How could we give the average investor access to these opportunities? We realised we needed to use the power of many to aggregate large amounts of capital and get a seat at the table with the big guys.

If someone wants to raise $50 million to grow their business, they don't care where the money comes from — they just want it. If they can pick up the phone, call Future Fund and say, 'I've got this great opportunity. You're going to make a heap of money out of it. We need a $50 million loan', and the Future Fund does its due diligence and goes ahead with the investment, that's much easier than calling 50 different people and asking each of them for a $1 million loan. It's one conversation rather than 50. This is why capital raisers always go to the lowest hanging fruit, which is the guys and girls with the deepest pockets. (I use 'capital raiser' as a catch-all term for companies or businesses looking for investment — anything from property developers to start-ups.)

And this is why we needed to find a way to have deep pockets, so that we would also start getting those calls. Our solution was to build a technology platform to aggregate average investors. (By the way, yes, our theory has proven correct: we receive those calls with the great opportunities now.)

So we had the idea. Next we needed to get to the nitty gritty job of building it. Our ambition for iPartners was a platform with 20000 direct investors (we are nearly there at the time of writing this book), which meant we needed a technology platform that makes the business scalable and makes life easy for investors.

> *We wanted to make buying alternative assets as easy as buying listed equities (shares), so that people would enjoy investing with us.*

We decided to make the minimum investment amount per trade through our platform small enough for investors to build their own diversified portfolio. The minimum investment is $10000, making it accessible for investors to dip their toes in the water.

The final thing we needed was to find and package interesting trades. We needed a competitive advantage in an area of alternative assets where there's not much competition, so we initially focused largely on doing non-property assets. (This choice in hindsight was a good one as we are now the market leader in this space.) Property assets are very commoditised and are becoming so prevalent that they are increasingly moving away from being alternatives. Coming from an investment banking background, we knew a lot about non-property opportunities, which gave us a point of differentiation from a product perspective (although if the risk-return equation looks good we still offer property assets as part of broader business — our first two trades were actually property ones). This, coupled with our uniqueness from a service perspective, meant we could give investors access to opportunities they couldn't get any other way.

It took us three months of meetings to get to this point of clarity. I had a conversation with my boss at UBS and he agreed on a strategy and exit plan for me. Then the rubber hit the road: Rob and I co-founded iPartners. We built a beta form of our tech platform with Norm King, got access to our first investment products through personal connections, hired lawyers to put the documents in place and wrap the products together, and started building our database of investors. When you launch a trade you want investors to know it's there, so a database is critical.

The starting point for our database was our networks of contacts in the finance industry. In my roles over the years I had built relationships with clients whose jobs it was to invest the firm's money. Many invested their own money as well, but as small, individual investors they'd never had access to alternative assets personally, so I contacted them to offer them the opportunity to do so. We were putting together trades that looked just like what they were investing in at an institutional level in their day job, but through us they could invest in them personally. Many jumped at the opportunity. So our initial investors were people we knew, and over time it grew from there.

Our first trade

The first trade we found, packaged and offered to our database was a property equity transaction. We found the trade through our existing networks. It was an opportunity to participate in a residential land subdivision project alongside the developer by buying equity in the specific project, with expected double-digit return on capital for investors.

We'd just launched the business and our beta technology was ready to go. We had 20 investors on our platform who had all given us money for this trade and provided us with critical feedback about how they loved the tech solution and the investor experience. We were just about to settle, but at the final point, right before the development application had been approved, a rare frog (yep, this is private markets) was found in the dam on the land.

Going ahead with this transaction would have generated revenue, which would have been great to start off our business, but we decided it wasn't an appropriate risk for our investors. (For trades like this we don't typically charge our investors any fees; instead we generate revenue by charging the developer for our service of providing capital.) With the presence of this rare frog, the project was bound to become a drawn-out process to obtain a final DA (development approval), with significant delays and cost blowouts. There would have been dam remediation and all sorts of complications, all of which would have reduced the returns. We didn't want to put our investors through that. We still had the option to walk away. Doing so was in the investors' best interest, so that's what we did, and we gave the investors their money back. We may have also saved a few frogs!

The investors loved it. They realised they could rely on us to represent their best interests above all else. We could have done the transaction and kept the revenue and it may or may not have been a good transaction, but by giving the money back we developed more credibility than if we'd done the trade. It built trust. Investors realised, 'These guys are real.'

This set the tone for how we run our business. We care a lot about relationships. We know our capital raisers need to get funding as low as possible, and our investors want a nice, risk-adjusted return. We've got to make both parties happy, because we want whatever asset we invest in to perform and be successful for our investors. We also need the capital raisers to make money, because that protects our investors.

> *Alternative assets and private markets are relationship-based businesses. Unless you build relationships and create win-win outcomes, you're going to struggle.*

We don't behave like the big investment banks who say, 'We're the big guys. You do what we say.' We're in the real world with real humans and real businesses. When we're dealing with capital raisers and investors, we put ourselves in their shoes, think through their situation and deal with the relationship as required.

I think growing up in a small country town, flunking HSC, playing sport, working at the gym and only slowly making the path into banking has helped me understand people, because it has exposed me to a broader range of people. I count myself lucky because I have great friends — not just in banking, but in construction, media, engineering, smelter factories and on farms. It gives me access to a spectrum of skills, personalities and viewpoints, and a vision of the world that I'm really grateful for.

I also think it helps that I've experienced living on a tight budget. I believe that when you're running the money for investors, you need to know the value of money. When you've lived on a limited budget, you value a dollar. I value a dollar. I wasn't born into comfort or financial ease. So when I run other people's money, I'm more cautious about risking that dollar. This does not mean I don't take risks. It means I ensure I have a very good understanding of the risk-return balance, the downside and how we can get our money back. As I said, a lot of the investors who backed us in the early days of iPartners were friends and colleagues. I knew them all. And, being raised in a country town where you pretty much know everybody means I look at my investors as though they are all friends and colleagues. I want to protect their money. I feel personally responsible for it. When they are investing through iPartners I am typically also investing alongside them with my own capital. It's how we came up with the name actually: 'I partner with you'!

Our second trade

The second trade Rob and I put together was a senior secured property loan.

What is a senior secured loan?

This type of loan is actually quite similar to a traditional home loan (mortgage). A senior secured loan means the lender is ranked first to get repaid and has an underlying asset as security. If the borrower defaults you've got first right to call on the security. (When you get a home loan, the bank holds a senior secured loan, with your house as security, meaning if you default, they get the house.)

It's also possible to provide a junior loan, but that means you're ranked second in the capital structure (meaning a higher probability of loss) if things go bad. And it's possible to provide an unsecured loan (with an even higher probability of loss), which ranks below the junior loan. This is when you literally have no security. I explain it all in more detail in chapter 6.

About 80 per cent of the credit trades we do today are senior secured investments as they are the position in the capital structure that have the highest probability of a positive outcome for investors. I also have to be very comfortable with the underlying asset, alignment with the borrower and legal documents that are in place to do otherwise. It's always a risk-return discussion.

For this trade we provided a senior secured loan for a new property estate. The security was a massive piece of land where the developer was planning to build 43 houses. As the senior secured lender, we initially had the raw land as security. Then, as construction took place, we also had all the improvements on the land. The investment was a good one. It had an 18-month maturity, paying investors north of 10 per cent per annum and their money returned in full.

What was exciting at this point was that we had now worked on a property equity and property debt trade. It has always been the business' ambition to offer investors a diversified pool of alternative assets. We were now on the path and starting to tick those boxes.

Pitfalls of investing in alternatives

Investing in alternative assets directly yourself means going out on your own, in the private markets, looking for opportunities. It's difficult because there's no public noticeboard advertising opportunities. Usually, capital raisers make calls to institutions or uber-wealthy families who they know can invest big bucks, and the small investor never even hears about the opportunity. Alternatives are ad hoc and not commoditised, and this usually makes them initially complex to understand. This complexity opens up opportunity. It also opens up risk, such as default risk, counterparty risk and legal risk, among others! It's a bit like the wild west at times.

The first thing you need to do in private markets is be very considered about who you are partnering with and providing capital to. In the private market, if you do find an investment opportunity, you are often dealing with a private company, and you will often have direct contact and a relationship with the CEO and other principals in the business. You will typically meet the CEO before you do a trade. You'll understand their business model and analyse all their financials. Whereas if you buy shares in Macquarie Bank, for example, the company itself doesn't really notice. Most investors have never met the CEO. You take for granted that they're running the company well if the share price goes up and running the company badly if it goes down. That's the primary feedback loop.

> *Personnel vetting and avoiding low-quality*
> *partners and deal flow is your*
> *number-one protection.*

Then you need to go through the documentation with a fine-tooth comb, both the initial offer and the final contract, and then try to tweak it all in the investor's favour. Let's look at all of this in more detail.

Who are you dealing with?

The first thing to watch out for is the experience of the people you're investing with. Investing with the wrong people is probably the number-one reason things can go bad. It's very easy for a capital raiser to pay a lawyer and a marketing company to get the prettiest document with an awesome sales message. Some even advertise investment opportunities on the radio, but this doesn't mean they know what they're doing. In fact if they are on the radio it's possibly a red flag!

Critically assess who is involved in raising the capital, before even researching the investment opportunity itself. My first protocol is to ask, do I know them? Do I like them? Australia is a pretty small market and it's easy for me because I know most people in the industry, and if I don't know them it's easy to find out who they are from other people I know. If they're coming to me for capital and I've never heard of them it is not a good start — they might just have come back from overseas, or they might be a start-up business. There are reasons why it might still be okay. But it is my first red flag.

You might not have a wide network in this industry, which means you need to thoroughly investigate the CVs and backgrounds of the CEO and CIO (chief investment officer in charge of investments). You can often check LinkedIn to find them. Have they worked in a similar industry at a large bank or large fund manager before? What's their track record and experience? What's their track record with similar investments in their existing firm, and other firms?

Make sure their specific experience is relevant to the asset they're offering you to invest in. That's very important because each asset class has unique characteristics. And it's when something goes bad that you need someone who really knows what they're doing. When things are going fine, you can virtually invest with anyone. It's like buying equities when the whole market is going up: you can be a superstar. It's when equities are going down and things are going badly that you wish you'd thought more about it. It's the same with alternative assets: when things go bad you need to be with the right team.

Thinking like an investor means asking who the humans involved are. And even if they check out but you just don't like them or get on with them, don't invest. I have significant control over the outcome for my investors in what we do at iPartners. If I need to constantly work with awkward or difficult people, or people I don't like, it makes everything harder. So I say no to those opportunities on the basis of the people involved.

To illustrate why it's so important to analyse the background and experience of people involved, let me tell you about a capital raiser who has recently been prominent in the papers. The head guy was awesome at marketing and advertising from what I could tell. He was on the radio and hosting conferences, and he raised a couple of hundred million dollars. The problem is that he has a marketing background (possibly some character flaws as well), not a finance background! Unfortunately, I don't think his investors will get much of their money back.

When I first set eyes on his product, I immediately thought, 'This is complete dogshit.' It was marketed as a low-risk, fixed-income product. But what he was actually doing was deploying the money into early-stage investments via a related entity loan, which is in fact a very high-risk unsecured investment. Yet he marketed it to investors as low-risk, fixed income! It didn't take long for investors to realise things were wrong and legal action was launched. If those investors had done some research, they would have quickly seen the guy didn't really have any finance experience whatsoever and his product had very obvious flaws in the documentation.

He was using a borrowed financial services licence. But unfortunately people didn't do their due diligence, were possibly misled and have been left high and dry, and in court trying to recover their money.

Australian Financial Services Licences (AFSLs)

Australian Financial Services Licences are used to regulate the industry. People who are starting up their own financial services businesses often hire someone else's AFSL. They become what's called a Corporate Authorised Rep (CAR) of the AFSL holder who is responsible for supervising and monitoring the financial services activities of their CAR. It's not a no to deal with someone hiring a licence, as there can be genuine business reasons to do it, but it is a flag to prompt further investigation.

It's also important to know who will be doing the legal work. Firstly, so that you have confidence their work will be high quality. And secondly, because if something goes wrong you want to be able to take action against the lawyers, so you want to make sure they've got deep pockets or good PI (professional indemnity) insurance. I won't typically invest in something if the business is not using top-tier legal firms. Second-tier legal firms can also be okay because those firms are risking their reputation, but you need to ensure they have deep pockets and will be there for you when things are going well and not so well.

Also look at who the auditor is, and who does the financial accounting. Are they reputable and reliable?

What to look out for in the initial offer documents

Before investing, you will typically receive an information memorandum, prospectus or some other form of offer or disclosure document, maybe directly or from your accountant, financial planner or adviser. This is a document on the specifics of the transaction (sometimes it's hard to tell what the specifics are in low-quality documents, but in theory they should be there). That document basically says, 'This is the investment. Do you want to participate in it?' Because alternatives are skewed towards larger investors, the minimum investment can be quite large — often a minimum of $1 million, or $5 million — so you need to review that document carefully to make sure you understand what you're buying, as well as the risk of it.

Here are some things to look out for, including some potential red flags.

Disclosed risks

Go straight to the risks part of the offer documents and understand what they are. A lot of investors get excited about headline returns, but sometimes these are formed purely from a theoretical mathematical model that will be achieved if 25 ducks line up. The real world behaves differently from the assumptions made in a mathematical model. The offer document might include an estimated rate of return of, for example, 'expected rate of 25 per cent IRR'. (IRR is the internal rate of return. The simplest way to think of IRR is the annual rate of return that an investment is expected to generate. It typically includes all cash flows and a final expected value.) Just because the expected IRR is 25 per cent doesn't mean it's how it will play out. Say it's a property development: the returns could be significantly worse (or maybe even better), or interest rates could go up, or it could rain for three months. Go through the specific risks in the offer document. And if you can't find the risk section in the documentation, or if it's a very short section — that's a very big red flag. Either they don't understand the risks, or they do understand them and haven't bothered to disclose them. Worst case, they're hiding the risks. Doesn't matter: not disclosing the risks in an offer document is misleading and a breach of the law. So don't invest.

Security

Another key thing to watch out for is security. If you're doing a loan, what is the underlying security? Often, investors will see a headline coupon (interest rate) that says 10 per cent return, but that 10 per cent could be a good or bad risk-return depending on what the security underlying that investment is. If the first thing you see promoted is the coupon in massive bold letters, they could be using the 'sex sells' approach, and you need to look deeper.

You really need to understand what the asset is that is being loaned against, and where you rank in capital structure (also known as the 'capital stack'). We will go into this in more detail in chapter 4, but for now, the simplest way to think of capital structure is that there is a hierarchy of loans, with those at the top having greater security but lower returns. Senior secured loans are at the top because they get paid out first. These have the lowest risk and the lowest return. Below that are junior secured and mezzanine loans. They get paid out next, after the senior secured loan, and have less security, therefore higher risk and higher expected return. Below that can be unsecured loans and equity-like capital such as convertibles or hybrids. Equities (shares) are at the bottom. (Shares are always the last to get paid out and might get nothing at all.)

The closer you are to the bottom of the capital structure, the less security you have. The less security you have, the more return you need to make it worth your while.

So remember: less security = more risk = higher rates of expected returns!

You need to be very careful on your security because if you think you are buying a senior secured position, and find after reading the final documents that you actually have a junior secured position (or even worse, no security), you will have a significantly higher risk trade than you wanted, which means you should be getting paid a higher return. Do not be influenced by higher interest rates. I would typically prefer a lower interest rate and my money back with a more attractive risk-return position, than a high interest rate and a worse risk-return position.

High fees

Examine the fees and ensure they're appropriately disclosed. If the fees seem too high, that's probably a bad sign. There are two primary ways an investment promoter generates fees: through charging the investor or charging the capital raiser. (Stating the obvious: it is better if the capital raiser pays as it's not a drag on investor expected returns.) If you, as the investor, are paying all the fees (instead of the capital raiser) then that eats away a large chunk of your return. Let's say the fees are 5 per cent on a one-year investment, and going through the documents you see that you're only getting a 7 per cent return out of the investment, this means the gross return is 12 per cent. You're taking a 12 per cent risk, but as an investor you are only getting 7 per cent out of it because someone else is taking 5 per cent in fees on the way through. This is a red flag as in this example you are paying away at 40 per cent of the expected return in fees. It might even be an okay investment from a risk perspective, but from a return perspective getting 7 per cent on something you should be getting 12 per cent on makes it a pretty bad trade.

It is appropriate for financial service providers to generate revenue — without it they wouldn't exist. Ultimately, everyone needs to make money. However, over the years I have learned that there are those with the ambition to make money quickly who will skew the equation in their favour with excess fees for a quick win. These are the types to avoid. A quick scan of the fee section will help you understand whether they are in the long game to benefit investors through building positive long-term relationships or the short game to benefit themselves with a fee grab!

The other key element of fees to understand is the fees you don't see, or which are not clearly disclosed. This is where I spend a lot of my time: trying to understand the real fees (the promoter's revenue), as these can drive behaviours and create conflicts.

Conflicted fees

In some types of trades, such as those offered by capital-raising businesses associated with property-development companies, there can be conflicts.

As an example, if one of these capital-raising businesses was offering an investment in a senior secured property loan paying 8 to 10 per cent per annum and they had disclosed reasonable fees in the offer documents, I would look at that and say on the surface it looks okay — not a great price on a historical basis, but okay.

What I would then do is dig a bit deeper into the capital raiser to see if there are associated entities involved. For example, if the loan was being used for a project where the sponsor (equity owner of the project) was an associated entity of the borrower, then it's a red flag because they are potentially incentivised to keep the interest rate on the loan (my investment) as low as possible as this would maximise the return on equity. A conflict exists because on top of the disclosed fee they are also making money through equity. Then I would want to look at who the developer is. Again, it could be an associated entity, which could mean that a developer margin is added to the project. If that is the case, they are also making money as the developer.

These are the types of investments and capital raisers that concern me the most as an investor, as they are dipping into a fee well multiple times. There is a lot of vertical integration in the business and this creates a lot of conflicts. So on top of the disclosed fees, associated entities to my loan investment are also generating a return on equity and a developer margin, which could easily be double-digit total project returns. This creates a pretty nice incentive for them to sell the debt to me!

In a worst-case liquidation scenario, who wins? Will the sale of the security (the property) for recovery of capital, which should benefit the senior secured lender, go ahead? Or will the project sponsor delay the sale of the security, benefiting themselves over the senior lender (my investment)?

My view is to avoid businesses where it is obvious that managing the conflicts is very difficult.

Vague promises about returns

Words such as 'expected', 'potentially' and 'targeted' are red flags because they are not definitive. For equity investments, it could be appropriate, because you don't know for sure how the business will go, but for investments that should have more defined expected outcomes, such as private credit, it would be a real concern to read 'targeted return' because it means what they're telling you is approximate. It's likely to be a marketing angle and the real information is possibly located somewhere else in the document (look for it) or not disclosed. In this situation, my first question to the promoter would be to ask for analysis on the expected range of return outcomes, from low to high. Breaking down a wide range of expected return outcomes to a midpoint single number can be misleading.

> **The next question to the promoter would be, 'How much are you investing?' If the answer is zero, that's another big red flag.**

If the promoter, who presumably has asymmetric access to information, is not investing, I often think, why would I? (Asymmetric access to information means that the promoter is putting the deal together, so they know *everything* about the deal. I only know the little bit they're telling me in the offer document. In other words, the promoter has access to a lot more information than I do. This is why it is asymmetric.)

Extensions and maturities

Maturity is the length of time the loan is for, or timing of the expected exit. Is it a fixed maturity, or is it callable (meaning you or the capital raiser can initiate the investment to end sooner)? Are there terms such as 'potential extension' (meaning the capital raiser has the right to extend the maturity)? For example, there could be an expected maturity of one year, but when you dig through the documents it actually says that under certain circumstances it will be extended at the borrower's choice up to an additional two years. If the return justifies this potential extension, that's fine. Just be aware that terms such as this exist and an expected maturity can end up being the 'expected' but not the actual in reality, so it's best to know up front, because you could be in the trade for a lot longer than you thought.

Ambiguous exit strategies

An exit strategy is one of the most critical parts of investing. Review how you exit the investment, and how you get your money back. The most important part of investing is getting a return; the second most important is getting your money back. (Arguably they are mutually equal first in importance.) Review the section on maturity. Is it a refinance? (Can it be refinanced? In a distressed market probably not.) Is it sale to a third party? (What is the certainty of a buyer? Always market and performance dependent.) Is it an IPO (initial public offering)? (Timing of IPOs is very volatile.) Whatever it is, you want to understand the probability of the exit occurring. The higher the uncertainty, the greater the expected return that I would be looking for. A clean, highly predictable exit typically suggests to me a lower risk.

Traps to be aware of

There are a number of traps you should be aware of before signing anything. Risks exist in every investment opportunity — which is why you get a return greater than 0 per cent — but this doesn't mean it's fine to take a cavalier approach. Due diligence and thorough risk assessment can highlight which investments are worth the risk they come with, and which most definitely are not.

Refinance risk

Refinance risk is a very genuine risk on a maturity date, particularly in private credit. If the capital raiser can't find another funder, say on a debt instrument, you may end up holding an investment longer than expected and that's something an investor needs to consider. ('Debt instrument' is a broad term that covers any number of loan structures. It can also be referred to as a 'fixed interest instrument'.)

As a simplistic example, let's say Big Bank has loaned you money for one year to purchase your home and after that year passes, Big Bank says, 'Give me my money back.' You say, 'I can't. I don't have the money because I bought a house.' You then chat to all of the other friendly banks to see if they will lend you the money so you can pay back Big Bank. That's refinancing. If the other banks say, 'We have no desire to lend you money!' then because you haven't been able to refinance the loan, Big Bank says, 'I'm not extending your loan because you didn't pay me interest or perform the way you needed to.' Big Bank would then have the right to take your house and sell it to get their money back. That's the consequence of not being able to refinance.

This is a simplistic example using a residential property. This refinancing risk is magnified in commercial property as there are typically larger amounts and more complex projects. If the asset cannot be refinanced, your investment exit is going to be extended, or your return will be negatively impacted.

In the investment scenario, your refinance risk of loss as a lender is considerably reduced if you're senior in the capital structure because you've actually got the asset as your security. Although, if you need to exercise on the security — sell the house — where you rank in the capital structure does not save you the time, legal costs, price impact and administration burden of having to take over the asset and force the sale in order to get your money back.

Counterparty risk

Be very careful of counterparty risk. The counterparty is the company you are doing the trade with. You want to be sure the counterparty has a ringfenced legal structure that avoids being polluted by losses on other assets; for example a unit trust, set up with a segregated trustee bank account that your investment will go into. This ensures that your investment never gets mixed up with the operations of the capital-raising company, which would expose you to substantially more risk. If the company folded, your money would become part of the assets in liquidation. If it is segregated in a special purpose company or trust, you will typically have more pure exposure to the underlying investment as the special purpose entity has one job, and that is to hold the underlying investment for your beneficial interest.

For example, we have iPartners Holdings, which is our operating company, and iPartners Nominees, a trustee. Every time we set up a fund, investors put money into the iPartners Nominees trustee bank account. Money then goes from the trustee bank account to purchase the asset (the investment).

When the borrower (assuming a loan asset) pays interest, it goes into the trustee bank account, and then to the investor. Because it's only going through a trustee's bank account and the trustee exists only to represent the interests of the unit holders, it never touches iPartners, the holding company. There isn't counterparty risk against iPartners because the money stays in the trustee account. If the money went via an iPartners Holdings bank account, that would be less desirable as it could get mixed up with the iPartners operating company, which you don't want. As an investor you want pure exposure to the underlying asset.

Operational risk

Operational risk is the risk that a good investment will go bad due to operational aspects (sloppy administration). You could invest with an awesome investment team who goes out and finds you the best investment opportunity, and it looks great on paper, but if the counterparty is a small business with no operations staff, or a medium-sized business lacking operational experience and expertise, things can go bad. Operational aspects include things such as making sure bank accounts are set up correctly, cyber security, payments are made to the right bank accounts, the right payments are made, payments are chased up and that the company is being run well operationally. This is particularly key if you are investing through a small firm of investment professionals because they are usually not great at administration. For most of their careers they have been doing investments working at big institutions, so they've always had someone doing the admin for them. If they haven't set the back office up along with an operations side of the business, things can quickly go wrong. They could forget to lodge a charge over security, or not onboard an investor properly, or make any other combination of administrative mistakes that could easily cost you money as an investor or impact their ability to stay in business and manage the investment for you.

Liquidity

There are two limbs to liquidity risk. The first is simply the length of the investment: if it's say two years with limited ability to exit before maturity (even for an emergency), this means it's illiquid because you can't get your money out when you need it. The second is the market liquidity for a given investment, meaning even though you can potentially liquidate (sell) your investment, you may not be able to get the price you want at the time you need to sell. You may be forced to sell at a distressed price due to the lack of liquidity (buyers) available near fair value. Any liquidity (buyers) in a crisis is better than none, so the second limb is typically the better of the two.

Legals, taxes and regulations

This one is largely out of the investors' control, although consideration should be given to things such as whether the investment has an aggressive or questionable tax benefit that drives a large proportion of the returns. If there's a possibility that the relevant tax legislation could change and/or be interpreted differently from how it's presented by the investment promoter, you could be left in a less favourable position. All sorts of regulatory or law changes are possible that could impact your investment. Development assets can be particularly sensitive to local government whims on zoning. The best an investor can do is use common sense, consider tax outcomes a secondary, not a primary, benefit, and stay on top of proposed or draft legislative or regulatory amendments (or invest with someone who will do it for them).

Market risk

Market risk is part of investing. Without it we would not get any return on our capital. These risks exist everywhere in investing and include credit, interest rate, currency, commodity and inflation, to name a few. They can be tolerated as part of investing with the understanding that with the risk comes the return, or you can attempt to isolate and hedge a particular risk. A simple example could be hedging an interest rate risk: you could buy a floating rate corporate bond (you receive a floating interest rate) and be happy with the credit and liquidity risk of the underlying bond, but be concerned interest rates may fall. You could hedge this risk through receiving fixed in an interest rate swap from a bank (who wants to pay a fixed interest rate) and you paying a floating interest to the bank, effectively removing the falling interest rate risk. This is achieved because the two floating legs cancel out, leaving you just receiving fixed in the interest rate swap, so then if rates fall you don't care because you are hedged. See figure 2.1 (overleaf) for a diagrammatic representation of this. I prefer not to hedge, primarily because hedging costs you money. The hedge counterparty will be clipping you a fee or margin, and as alternatives are illiquid, hedging risk in general tends to be more expensive. I prefer to invest on the merits of the asset and consider the risk-return as a package as part of a longer term diversified alternative allocation, and part of that is getting paid to take interest rate risk.

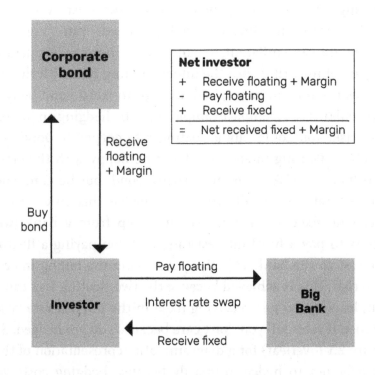

Figure 2.1   Interest rate swap

Business risk

This is a similar risk to market risk, although it is more a consideration of the day-to-day risks of investing at the operating business level. General market conditions can impact the performance of a business. This risk is more idiosyncratic in that management can underperform, struggle to hire staff, find finance or back the wrong widget, among other things. (We will go through this in more detail in chapter 6, but for now, be aware that exposure to a single company is a very concentrated investment; if the business performs well you win, if not you lose. My preference is to invest through a pooled, diversified type of structure where I can minimise single asset exposure. There is a place for single business investing, such as providing growth capital to an emerging business, although because it is higher risk–higher return, as investors we need to be aware that we could lose our entire capital. If you do enough of these, it is certain it will happen at some point, so size your investment as such — that is, invest smaller amounts because you know at some stage you'll lose in this early-stage, emerging business). Later-stage, single-business investments have lower business risk than early-stage. On the positive side, if the company flies, the upside is very exciting!

Fraud

This is the risk that makes me the most nervous in private markets because it is virtually impossible to hedge. It's unpredictable and typically terminal when it occurs. As investors, the only real protection is working with an investment platform where investors' interests are aligned with the manager's. The best protection is the due diligence process, which platforms such as iPartners conduct as a matter of form. This includes background checking, reference checking and analysing their track record. It is through this approach you can filter out known bad eggs, or questionable eggs, and not do the trade. The next stage is the diligent ongoing monitoring, digging into the monthly reports, reviewing bank statements to identify issues early and take action. However, there is no perfect answer to protecting yourself against criminals! So investing with people you can trust is always paramount.

Conflicts

The main conflicts that occur for an investor are between you and the promoter of an investment opportunity, primarily because they will generate fees from your investment, and then also between you and the capital raiser, as your capital will likely allow them to generate an above-average return if successful. This conflict will always exist in investing (it's unlikely anyone is offering a service for free). What is most important is how the risk is addressed, but in short, the primary way you should expect this risk to be addressed is to ensure there is a fair alignment of interest among all parties and some independent oversight. If this doesn't exist, it could well be a red flag and a trade to walk away from.

COVID-19

Enough said! It impacts lots of things, but pretty much a common-sense approach is required to consider knock-on implications of this one. Hopefully this will fall out of the risk section eventually.

And the list goes on...

This can go on forever. A good investor document will disclose the major relevant risk clearly and concisely for you to understand, although the list could theoretically be endless: 'Web3 blows up the internet, satellite hitting earth risk...'

The ones above are typically worth considering and scanning to understand, although if none of these are disclosed it would feel like a red flag, as I would typically expect some of these to be relevant in the alternative asset space.

Strategies for success

Investing is not easy — otherwise everyone would be doing it! There are many things you can do in private markets that have less to do with the investment and more to do with the approach. Here are a few insights on how I go about the softer side of investing and trying to balance the outcomes in my, and my investors', favour.

Start small

The first time you invest with a particular group, invest less than you want to. Start small. Even if they've passed every level of your analysis — for example, they've got great CVs, you've compared them to others, fees are fair — I recommend only investing a small amount on your first investment.

Let's say the investment has a 12-month maturity, and even though you want to put in $40000, if it was me, I'd put in half that to start. There's always another investment down the road. Invest half, and see what happens. Did you get your first coupon (interest payment)? How was their reporting? Do they provide enough information? Is the asset performing as was written on the box? If you have a good investor experience, you might want to invest a little more next time. Over time you'll work out which are good, credible groups to back and which are not.

You actually never want to put too much into one trade. That's the driver from an iPartners perspective. We make the minimum small so that you can make those choices and diversify your own portfolio over time.

Make sure interests are aligned

A key thing to understand is alignment of interest. This is all about ensuring that, if things go badly, someone else loses money or feels pain before you do. The benefit of someone else losing money before you do is that this person, or group of individuals, is going to work really hard to ensure *they* don't lose money (unless they're nuts), so it's a way to reduce the chance of a bad outcome in your investment as they will be focused on protecting their own.

What you really want is for that person or group of people who could lose money before you to be the owner of the business: the person who will profit most from the business's success and a positive outcome. Alignment of interest in a structural way means that everyone protects everyone else out of self-interest. That person or group will, out of self-interest, protect themselves from losses, and by default that includes protecting you because they're subordinate to you in some way, shape or form.

A great example to explain how this works in practice is how iPartners structured our investment with an education lender. This trade, which matured long ago (although we continue to work with them to this day on capital solutions, further highlighting that private markets are all about partnerships), was one of the earliest trades we put together for investors.

Example of alignment of interest

An education lender came to iPartners and said, 'We're passionate about education and we want to provide loans to parents with children in private school as a cash management tool.' (They have proven this over time as well.) A lot of schools make you pay up-front fees for the full year, and they wanted to lend the money up front for parents to pay back monthly. But they needed capital to do this.

We said, 'We're happy to lend you some money, but we need to ensure there's a strong alignment of interest and that we've got the right security in place. If you put all of your equity into this investment vehicle, as first loss or subordination below us, then we'll put in place a secured loan to help you lend money to parents of private school kids.' What this meant is, say there's a $10 million portfolio, they need to put $2 million cash into this vehicle, and we then put in our $8 million investment senior to that, which means if there are any losses they'll lose money before we do.

The thinking behind this is that they're going to work really hard to run their business well because they're not going to want to lose their money. And this protects our investment.

With this client we set it up as a two-year investment that paid quarterly interest. From their side, they give money to parents, and the parents pay principal and interest to them as they pay off the loan. That's the revenue for them. Then they

(continued)

pay us interest for our loan, which is their business expense. (And they, of course, make money because the interest rate they charge the parents is higher than what they pay us.)

Alignment of interest only exists when it's structured correctly into the legal documentation, with controls, to make sure investors are protected. The terms we got into our documentation with them meant that they and the investors were completely aligned. If they didn't perform, we had controls in place in the documentation to apply pressure on them. These were monetary incentives, and are another core part of creating alignment.

What are monetary incentives?

An example of monetary incentives is reserving some of the capital raiser's profits, and not releasing them until they either perform or give us our money back. Reserving their profits creates alignment of interest with us as the lender because they want the profits for themselves, so they'll do what it takes to ensure performance. Including this right to reserve profits in the documentation gives the investor extra protection, and you usually set performance triggers for when this is enacted and/or released. Then, if things start to go poorly in the company, you can simply say, 'Well, the net interest margin, which is the profitability of your business, is going to stay in the company. It's not going to get paid out to you. It will stay as emergency money, a reserve to cover any losses that come through, to ensure our investors get their interest and their money back.' This is all in the legal terms that are written in. It creates great alignment of interest because they'll work extra hard to get you your money back so that their profit is released.

With this client we made sure they put their equity down as first loss as above, and we also created a monetary incentive by requiring them to keep 25 per cent of their profits in the company until our investors were repaid. We also structured the trade so that if there was a loss in their portfolio and the performance was deteriorating, we would keep 100 per cent of their profit in that vehicle until they gave us our money back. Credit to them: they performed and none of these clauses were called into play, which is the key to structuring investments. You always plan for the worst-case scenario. If it never occurs, then perfect, but if it does occur you are very happy the protection clauses exist.

You put these in place by having them as legal terms in your documentation. The legal structure we created for our trade with the educational lender was unique and the first of its kind in education. It has since been replicated in many other iPartners trades.

INVESTMENT STRUCTURES — THE BIG GUYS

Another way to align interests is via investment structures (more on these shortly). You get alignment of interest by having big, deep-pocketed investors who put their capital in alongside you.

Say the Future Fund is investing with us (they aren't, but it's useful for the example), and you go and invest alongside them. It's a pretty nice alignment of interest, right? The Future Fund has a couple of hundred staff members analysing investments, and you know that whatever returns they get, you're also going to get. Aligning with some bigger, institutional fund managers who have deeper pockets means you can leverage off the due diligence they do. Just ensure that whoever your fund manager is, or whoever you're investing with, is actually putting some of their capital at risk too. In some cases they may be originating an asset for a fee then selling it down to another investor, so not taking any net exposure or risk. If you ask a fund manager how much they've got in and the reply is zero, I'd get pretty nervous. If they're not prepared to put their money in, why should you? That's alignment.

The staff within iPartners, and I personally, invest in the transactions that we bring to market. We personally put our money in because we want these returns for ourselves too. For the investor sitting there wondering, 'Look, do I want to put my $50000 in?' it probably gives them comfort to know that I'm putting some of my money in too. If it goes up, we all win, and if it goes down, we all lose. This is called 'having skin in the game'. Having skin in the game is a critical part of funds management investing in general. My colleagues and I don't get any more favourable terms than our investors: we're investing with them. This is a perfect example of our interests being totally aligned.

It's why we're called 'iPartners', of course!

Investment structures

I'm going to run through the most common legal structures we come across locally, in case you're interested in digging deeper into investment structures.

There are lots of different ways to offer investments in Australia. Sometimes the decision can be about tax efficiency; other times it's simply scalability of documentation. This is something we focus on a lot at iPartners as it keeps the legal fees down (less drag on investor returns) and makes it simpler for investors. (We use consistent legal structure

---

and drafting where we can, which makes it easier for our investors to read through the documentation.)

Note structures

These tend to be a debt instrument issued from a special purpose company or trust (in theory, a bankruptcy remote type issuer), with some type of security trust arrangement to ensure the investor risk is linked to an underlying asset, or pool of assets, rather than the issuer. Investors would typically receive an information memorandum (IM) surrounding the note program and a term sheet or pricing supplement to highlight the specifics of the investment.

Corporate bonds

This is another debt instrument, with the most common type being senior bonds issued by companies, where investors directly take on the credit risk of the issuing entity. Most of these would be considered part of the public market, intermediated largely by banks and financial institutions. There would tend to be a program prospectus or an IM as disclosure documents and an attached pricing supplement or term sheet for the new issuance.

Unit trusts

The most common issuance structure for private markets in Australia is the unit trust. Investors will own the units, which pass through the economics of the underlying assets directly to investors. A unit trust could also issue a note. There tends to be limited discretion by the trustee because through the trust deed, all assets are allocated on a fixed proportion to each unit holder. Investors would tend to receive an IM that bundles all of the disclosure information together with the trust deed or alternatively

(continued)

discrete documents such as the trust deed, conditions and a term sheet as separate documents.

Deferred purchase agreements

Deferred purchase agreements (DPAs) have a long history in the structured product market, first starting with zero + call type structures. They are financial contracts between two parties where you as the investor agree to receive an asset on maturity of your investment (deferred purchase) rather than cash (e.g. shares). The amount of the asset you receive on maturity depends on the performance of an underlying reference asset for the duration of your investment, which could be an index, basket of shares or various investment strategies. Although this is a bi-lateral contract, investors would typically receive an IM.

Derivatives

A derivative is also a financial contract between two parties with the value of the contract derived from the performance of an underlying asset, such as an index, shares, commodities, currency or interest rates. The most common type of derivative is an option. It can be executed under the ISDA regime (this is an internationally agreed standard master document for derivatives transactions, in theory designed to simplify the documentation process, although in my experience, negotiating an ISDA is a mess of lawyers trying to win points that takes months!) or packaged into a long-form contract, PDS or IM.

Sub-participation agreements

These tend to exist mostly in loan transactions. You will not be the lender of the record (the lender who is recorded on the loan agreement) or a party to the loan transaction. You will invest via a contract (sub-participation) that is designed to pass the economics on the underlying transaction through to you. It can increase the risk to an investor as you will have indirect exposure and full risk to the borrower, with likely no control over the security as you are relying on someone else (the lender of record) to act in your best interests. You also have an additional risk of an exposure to the party to the contract (the grantor of the sub-participation). The key in this situation is to ensure alignment of interest and risk participation by the grantor and lender of the record.

Ensure your documentation is watertight

Documentation is absolutely critical. Every transaction in private markets is different. If you get your documentation wrong, things can end very badly.

All of the terms need to be accurately drafted. Things like dates, interest amounts, capital amounts, coupons, security, maturity dates, call dates... all of these key economic elements are critical in the documentation. If you key 'four years' instead of 'three years' into a legal document — because fat fingers happen — then suddenly the investment looks very different. If it gets signed as four years when you wanted it for three years, you'll get to three years and ask for your money back because you think the investment has matured. They can reply, 'Actually, you signed up for four years.' That little fat finger means you've taken on an exposure that can actually be very different from what you thought you had.

If you forget to put in a clause that creates an alignment of interest, and a loan is underperforming, there's nothing you can do. If you call them to say, 'Actually, we agreed that you would give us all of your profit when you're underperforming', their response could be, 'There's something here on email about that, but the final agreement we signed doesn't have that clause.'

It's critical to ensure that the legal terms are documented in detail using a reputable legal firm. If something goes wrong you don't want to be using a small legal firm, because ultimately you want to have recourse to them, and the ability to sue them if needed. In my eyes, this is why you must always use middle-to-large-sized legal firms. You aren't necessarily always paying for their skill; you're paying for the balance sheet as well if something goes wrong. You need someone who's prepared to stand behind their advice if things go wrong.

If you don't complete a permitted action drafted in the documentation, you can get yourself in hot water. For example, let's say the documentation states that you can register a charge because you loaned money to a company to do a property development and they've given you security over a piece of land and bank accounts. ('Charge' effectively means taking a security interest [legal claim] that in the case of default gives you control over particular assets.) If you (or your lawyers) forget to register the charge with, for example, the Land Registry or PPSR (Personal Property Security Register) after you've loaned the money, you actually have no security whatsoever. You've got a legal document (assuming you've signed one) that gives you the rights, but if you haven't registered that security and actioned your right, you're completely unsecured and will need to scramble to fix it, although it may be too late by then. They could have gone ahead and got another loan from another party, provided the same security, and then that person would rank ahead of you because they registered the charge. This has happened to people! It's so important to do the 'boring bits' — the documentation — diligently.

If you get your documentation wrong, even the best transaction will give you a different outcome and consequently a different rate of return from the one you expected.

Example of documentation being wrong

There are some public cases of things going wrong because of mistakes or misinterpretation in documentation. For example, there's a case with an Australian oil and gas company. It was a convertible note and in there was a material disagreement in the interpretation of the documentation between parties. The investing party had a view that the notes could be converted into shares at a ratio of 6.6 ordinary shares for each convertible note, whereas the company had a view the notes were convertible to shares at a ratio of one ordinary share for each convertible note. The investors ended up getting a significantly outsized return on their capital purely because of this clause and the company ultimately agreeing to a settlement. The company sued a large local legal firm, presumably to recoup some of those losses. It was quite a public case at the time as the larger investors were very vocal in their approach to investing in listed entities.

There are lots of less public incidents of documentation errors having material implications. The moral of the story: get your documentation right and use a lawyer you can sue if need be!

Understand the power of correlation

Correlation is a measure of the relationship between two investments. Correlation is positive when they both move together (up or down) and negative when one investment falls at the same time as the other rises.

Correlation is a very useful thing to understand, so that you can build the most efficient portfolio from a risk-and-return perspective. Everyone talks about diversification in investing, which is literally about diversifying your risks so you're not concentrated in only one asset (the old adage: 'don't put all your eggs in one basket'). If you have $100 to invest and you buy equities, and equities go down 20 per cent, you lose $20. If equities go up, you make $20. You're 100 per cent exposed to equity. It's got a correlation of one.

Most people would say, 'You have to diversify your money because if equities are down 20, that's bad.' So people will buy a bit of fixed income, maybe some commodities, and other asset classes, to diversify.

The statement is mostly correct, although I will use an extreme example of correlation to highlight that diversification alone is not valuable. Let's say you buy 50 per cent fixed income and 50 per cent equities and the correlation of fixed income to equities is also 1.0. If equities are up, you would expect your fixed income to be up in value; if equities are down, you would expect your fixed income to be down as they are perfectly positively correlated. So we have diversified in the traditional sense, although as the correlation is equal to 1.0, on a portfolio basis we have not really reduced risk or changed the return profile as the assets are moving in perfect unison, so we need to consider correlation to actually turn the diversification dial.

However, where it becomes more interesting and closer to a real-world example, if the behaviour of fixed income has a correlation of 0.5 to equities, that means whatever movement in equities occurs is about 0.5 for bonds. This means that if I had 50 per cent of my money invested in equities, and 50 per cent in bonds, and the equities market went down by 20 per cent, my $50 in equities is now worth $40, and my $50 in bonds is worth $45 (assuming correlation roughly holds up) because bonds have half the sensitivity to equities. So it's better than 100 per cent equities, and I am now getting some benefits of diversification, but the positive correlation still leads to correlated losses and gains.

Equities and bonds: what's the difference?

An equity is when you own part of the company's ordinary shares and have an uncertain expected return, whereas a bond is a form of debt—you lend money to the company and expect a defined return, such as the date that you will be repaid and how much interest you would expect to earn.

Correlation becomes really cool when there's a correlation of less than zero. In a perfect world you'd be adding assets that have a lower correlation. Say you had an asset with a −0.5 correlation to equities, meaning if the equities go down the other asset goes up. If the other asset goes down, equities go up. It's negatively correlated.

If fixed income had a correlation of −0.5, and equities went down by 10 per cent, I would expect my fixed income would actually be up by 5 per cent, which is a great situation from a portfolio perspective because I've partially hedged my equity position by adding fixed income. Correlation is critical in creating a more diversified and efficient portfolio.

Alternative assets tend to have low to negative correlation to traditional assets, meaning they behave differently. They tend to go down or up or stay the same at different times, which makes your portfolio a lot more robust. That's sort of the basic logic of correlation.

Alternative assets are the most interesting to add to a portfolio from a low correlation perspective, pushing out the efficient frontier (which is basically a theoretical portfolio that has the most attractive risk and return across all available assets). For example, during the beginning of the COVID-19 pandemic when equities were down around 30 per cent, the iPartners Investment Fund was still worth roughly the same as before (due to the shorter duration and contractual nature of private credit returns). So if you'd had half your portfolio in this credit fund, which has had a historic return of between 9 per cent and 10 per cent a year, and half in equities, you wouldn't have lost as much. That is the power of low correlation investments and the contractual returns available in private credit, which will be discussed in detail in chapter 6.

Investing in private markets gives you control

Back to my example about the Macquarie CEO you can't get access to. This means you have zero control. You've invested in Macquarie under the hope they do well, and you have no control over decisions they make or how they do (as a shareholder, strictly you can vote at general meetings, although as large chunks of the companies are owned by large fund managers, your vote is typically useless!). The largest fund managers or investment bank analysts could possibly call the CEO of Macquarie and have a cry about something, but anyone outside that close audience has zero access to management. You've got no control or access to changing the legal structure. It is literally a listed Australian equity that follows Australian equity rules. All you can do is buy and sell the stock.

In comparison, if you invest in equity or debt in a private company, you have great access to management. When a company I'm negotiating with sends me a term sheet about what they want to achieve, I can go back to them and say, 'What you've asked for is okay, but it doesn't really gel with what I like. I'd like this, this and this, and we're going to document it. I want a lower valuation on your business and better terms on the entry. I want to use my lawyers to document it like this because that's how we do things and it's more efficient.' (I am nicer than that, but you get the point.) During that iteration process I have total control over the legal structure. I have reasonable control over the economics and financial structure and I also have great access to all their financials, business modelling, the board and their staff. I can visit their premises and influence their decision making. That level of control only exists in private markets.

The control continues after I end up investing. If everything went fine, I might say, 'I want to have a seat on your board. I've given you enough equity and I actually want some control.' We tend not to do this, but I could say it to them or have the right to take a board seat. If they're underperforming, I could pick up the phone on a Saturday morning and call them to say, 'What's going on? I need an update, put me through to your CFO.' Again, I don't often do that, but the information is on tap. It's a partnership. They know they need our capital, and they probably want more as they grow. If they perform, we might invest more, so they really want to impress us and see us as a partner because we're a part of the journey.

If things are going badly, aside from that access, I can make them do things. If it's a debt instrument, I can say, 'Well, you're not taking on any more debt now. Or you need to ask me for approval before you do things, or you need to start amortising.' (Amortising debt simply means the principal is repaid over time, typically to a repayment schedule, so it reduces the debt outstanding, in theory reducing the risk.)

It's important to be very assertive to make sure things are skewed our investors' way, while being respectful to the capital raiser. That level of control is so valuable for investors.

What your friendly financial planner will advise you to do

When you go to your friendly financial planner for advice, they'll recommend an Australian equity fund in your portfolio. Then they'll suggest an international equity fund, a property trust allocation, a fixed-income bond allocation and cash. I'd say 80 per cent of financial planners will give you some version of that recommendation when you see them. They will tweak the weights depending on your age and risk profile, income, and so on, but without a doubt, that's what you're going to get in your portfolio.

If you're a self-directed investor your choice is pretty much to go to an online broker and buy listed equities or approach fund managers directly to purchase their funds. Your choices are limited in the real world.

If you come to a platform such as iPartners, you can use the online broker (or your friendly financial planner) for direct equities and the traditional assets, but you can come to us and see it as a one-stop shop with all sorts of different assets you typically would not be able to have access to. You've now got choice. You can buy property debt and equity, asset-backed debt, venture capital, corporate loans, part of a pub, part of a piece of land. You could buy part of a dairy farm. All of these quirky assets are available in lots of $10000 or more. The minimum investment for our investors is $10000, and that's very deliberate.

> *We want as many people as possible to be able to access alternative assets, and we want them to be able to invest in increments that suit their personal wealth.*

The lower you can make that minimum investment amount, the more choice they have.

They might have $100000 to invest across 12 months, so they could put $10000 in 10 different investments and build themselves a diversified portfolio of alternative assets that they historically would never have been able to access via any traditional wealth channel.

Globally, alternative platforms have enhanced the access to alternatives. In Australia, iPartners is the market leader.

Seven steps for finding the best trades

The Australian financial markets are so small that I am lucky enough that lots of people know me, and I usually know them. My first year running iPartners involved a lot of chasing existing contacts to find good investment opportunities, but now I have people contact me. In the past I'd maybe speak to a second-tier accounting firm, but now I get deals presented to me from large debt and equity advisory firms.

Still it's never easy to grow quickly. At the time of writing, to satisfy investor demand I expect to source around $750 million of new investments in the next 12 months (with an expectation to be approaching $6 billion of total assets on the iPartners platform). We did around $250 million last year, which means the business needs to find $500 million more high-quality opportunities to keep up with the growth of our platform and the demand for investment. Lucky for me, putting together trades is fun — it's the best part. A capital raiser will turn up with a problem, and I have to use my brain to creatively solve the puzzle and make an asset investable. That's the bit I like.

My model is investor driven. I'm not selling the investment opportunities; I'm simply saying, 'Here they are', outlining all the details, and letting investors decide for themselves. Typically I am co-investing too — we all love investing our own personal money into these opportunities.

Here's a step-by step process of how to find and execute trades.

Step 1: Finding investment opportunities

The market now knows it can source capital from me, so I'm one of the first calls when people are looking for capital. In any given week I might have 20 opportunities come across my desk. These come in through various channels, either to me personally, other staff or gatekeepers. I also haven't lost the fun of chasing down opportunities I see in the papers, on LinkedIn, in competitors' deals and through word of mouth. Just think of it as a huge funnel filling up with lots of opportunities (although a large portion of them are average and immediately deleted, so maybe it's a large funnel with a few holes in it to push some of the bad ones out the sides).

Step 2: Assessing opportunities

Usually I can quickly say 'no' to 80 or 90 per cent of those opportunities without too much work, narrowing it down to three or four opportunities that look promising and are worth exploring. The best skill to have is the ability to quickly say 'no' to average and bad trades. Otherwise so much time is wasted.

I have a soft side to filtering transactions, which is just as important as the numbers, facts and figures.

Soft skills

If I don't like the people, I don't proceed. It's amazing how powerful that gut feeling is of whether you like people or not. It's easy to work out if you get a bad vibe. Gut feelings are important when people seem to be bullshitting you or don't know their facts, or if they change the facts when probed. You can also read personalities. You can see if they're humble, driven and motivated: those traits are critical. It's nearly as easy to tell if they are stretching the truth or overselling.

Whether I know the people is a big indicator as well. If I get shown an interesting-looking transaction from someone I've never heard of, I'll speak to a few market contacts and try to find out if anyone knows of them. If not, it's typically a bad sign as Australia is a small market. So that can help me make a quick decision to say no to a bunch of opportunities.

The figures

I also quickly read the summary of the opportunity, do a scan analysis of the numbers and facts, then contrast it to similar deals, and it's quickly very clear which ones are definitely not worth pursuing and the ones worth further investigation.

Assessing seed capital

Seed capital is capital for a business that's still in the concept stages. It's harder to assess these opportunities because there's nothing really in existence yet and often the individuals are unknowns. But I usually get a pretty clear picture from having a discussion with them. For example, I recently had a call with a group who are trying to start a carbon-related business. Companies can buy carbon offsets, which means their consumer goods are carbon neutral. On the phone I started asking some questions and quickly realised they knew nothing about the industry. They had a good idea, but they clearly didn't know their market. They started stuttering and falling over their own answers. This might still be okay, because when people start a business they only half-know what they're doing, and they may have been nervous, so I have empathy for them not being experts. But it was still a red flag and very easy to decide to discard that opportunity or suggest they come back at a later date once the business is more evolved.

Step 3: Initial due diligence

Once I have narrowed the list down to the potential investments, our capital markets origination team does a desktop analysis that takes between half a day and a day. We'll look at the numbers, assessing if it's debt, equity or hybrid in nature. Then we'll look at issues of risk. What's the underlying risk? What's the offset to those risks? How do we ensure that we're going to get our money back? Is it profitable? Assets? Growth? Security? Essentially, we try to work out what could go wrong and once we know what could go wrong, we assess whether the upside seems commensurate with the risk.

Once we've worked through the underlying risk, we compare it to similar trades we've done in the past and how we priced those, which gives us some more context.

After this initial due diligence we get it down to two or three trades that have potential.

Step 4: Detailed due diligence

I then enter detailed due diligence, which is both a qualitative and quantitative analysis.

I go back to the people seeking capital and ask for their financials for the last three years (if applicable), their organisational charts and their key management CVs. I also get them to complete a due diligence questionnaire, which has around 100 questions on everything from personnel involved, operational risk, company risk, business risk and every sort of risk you can think of.

In this period it's typical to have what is called a data room, where they provide as much company data as possible in an attempt to predict my questions with answers to save everyone time. This is where I dig into all that information. If the capital raisers are any good they'll already have it set up — if they don't, it's a red flag or they may be just a little early in the process to be engaging me. If they aren't able to get the information to me quickly, maybe it's because they don't have the internal processes or systems. This can also be a red flag.

Once I've done this deep due diligence on two or three companies, there's usually one investment opportunity that stands out and has roughly the right numbers.

Next, I prepare a detailed paper for the investment committee. Our investment committee consists of our senior managers and most experienced investors and includes the co-founders

(Rob and me), the COO, head of capital markets business, head of legal, head of funds management and other members by invitation if specialist input is required.

The investment committee reviews the scope of papers and meets to discuss the appropriateness and quality of the trades. Again, the question for the investment committee, aside from content and fundamentals of the trade, is, 'Would you invest your personal capital?' If the answer is no, it will invariably not pass the committee. If it's not good enough for us, it's not good enough for our investors. This is the first scan by the committee with nothing approved at this stage.

Step 5: Negotiating the term sheet

Once the trade is approved in substance by the investment committee, the next step is to produce a draft term sheet (preliminary offer) and deal structure. I will make an opening offer of the terms I think will work for this transaction. Then I enter an iterative process of improving the term sheet in my favour, while respecting the capital raiser's interests and objectives. The capital raiser wants the money as cheaply as they can get it, and the investors want to get the biggest return they can for the risk, so we both go into battle to get the terms we want. There are many financial levers we can tweak to negotiate terms that get the best returns for our investors.

For example, if we put in a mandatory term that they don't like, I can offer something back, such as increasing the maturity or adding a call date. You try to never say no as it's ultimately a partnership. You try to say, 'Well, if it doesn't work, what about variables A, B and C?'

> *You try to get to a win-win scenario,*
> *as much as possible.*

Let's have a look at some of the levers we can use to negotiate.

Valuation

The valuation of the private company for equity investments is critical and that's where most of the negotiation happens. To any given amount of investment, I want to maximise how much of the company we own. We can do this through negotiating the company's value.

If they come to me and say, 'Our company is worth $10 million. Do you want to put in $3 million?' that means it's worth $10 million before I put money in and $13 million after I put money in. If you do the maths, with the $3 million I gave them, I now own 23 per cent of their business. But I want to own more of the business for the money I put in. So I'll say, 'I like your business and I see you've got a lot of potential. I think investors will like it. I can get you your $3 million to help your business grow. But I think, as of today, your business is not worth $10 million. I think it's worth $5 million as it's similar to this other business with a like valuation [or some other qualitative or quantitative assessment on value].' If you redo the maths, after I give them the $3 million, the business is valued at $8 million. This means I get 37.5 per cent of the company for my $3 million.

How is LVR (loan-to-value ratio) calculated?

Let's use some simple figures to make it easier to follow how the LVR is calculated. If I'm lending $70, and they offer $100 of security against that $70 loan, that means there's a $100 asset that I'm lending $70 against. That's a 70 per cent LVR (which is also referred to as 'lending 70c in the dollar').

Asset valuation is also critical for debt investments. Property in particular is heavily driven by LVR (loan-to-value ratio).

The higher the LVR, typically the higher the risk. So if a borrower says a piece of land is worth $100 million and they want to borrow $50 million, it's a 50 per cent LVR project. Although, say I get an independent valuation that suggests the property is worth $75 million, then the $50 million loan I was considering is now actually a 67 per cent LVR, which is significantly higher risk than initially considered.

NOT ALL VALUATIONS ARE EQUAL

Something to be very careful of when considering investing in property debt is the definition of the current valuation. Some investment promoters will refer to the completion valuation as if completed (even though the project hasn't even started) and others the 'as is' valuation, which is the property valuation today.

Ideally, you always want to use the 'as is' valuation because in the event of a fire sale what it is currently worth today is really the only security you have. The problem with investing on the basis of an LVR relative to completion value as if completed is that the LVR will be significantly higher compared to the 'as is' valuation. As an example, say a piece of land is worth $25 million on an 'as is' valuation and $50 million on a completion valuation and the proposed property loan is $25 million. On an 'as is' valuation the LVR is 100 per cent (very risky, equity-like risk) and the on-completion as if completed valuation LVR is 50 per cent (seems less risky, but misleading). I would personally ignore the completion valuation most of the time as it's not a great reflection of the real risk.

Maturity

Typically a borrower wants a longer maturity and an investor wants a shorter maturity. The investor can't predict what will happen in three years, but they can (sort of) predict what will happen in a year. Investors thus tend to be biased to the short term.

Let's say the capital raiser wants to borrow the money for five years, but I only want to lend it for two. They might come back with a counteroffer of three, at which point I might bargain by saying, 'You can have it for three, but I want to start amortising the debt from 18 months.' Amortising means that I start getting paid back before the three-year point. It's all about playing with the terms to get a nice product for investors, and trying to get something that's balanced for the capital raiser too.

On equity-like investments the exit is less in your control. You might expect an exit in five years, but the challenge is to judge the validity of the strategy relative to the expected exit, which is a rough science. In general, an exit date of five years realistically means an exit at five-to-seven years, as company owners or founders tend to be overly optimistic. You always want to be sure that the exit strategy is a valid one; otherwise your investment is potentially stuck and likely illiquid.

Call option

A call option is often added to debt instruments to give the capital raiser some flexibility. It is the right, but not the obligation, for the capital raiser to pay out the loan before the maturity date, which is something they might want to do if their company is performing better and they can get cheaper finance elsewhere. I prefer to lock them in for the length of the loan, because if I do the work to set up the trade I want to get paid across the agreed time frame. But I might give them the right to call the debt after 12 months in return for some other term that suits me, such as a higher interest rate.

Security

Security, as highlighted in prior chapters, is often expressed as the LVR in property.

If I am not happy with the security they are offering, because the LVR is too high, I might negotiate a higher interest rate to compensate. Or maybe I'll split the loan into a junior and senior loan with two different interest rates, and two risk profiles. (We'll look more deeply into junior and senior loans in part 2.) Say I am happy to make the loan at 70 per cent LVR (70c in the dollar) but they want 75 per cent (75c in the dollar). I might say, 'If you pay me 15 per cent interest, then 75 per cent LVR is okay.' Or I'll say, 'Let's do the 70 per cent loan, and how about I do a separate 5 per cent junior loan and I charge you 20 per cent for that? Your total loan is 75 per cent but I've given you two loans.' This allows two different risk profiles for investors to choose from. You have to think about every single variable, so you can come to a compromise point that seems fair for both parties.

Step 6: Investment committee review

Once we agree on a term sheet and both parties are happy and feel it will work, there's another committee review.

By the time a trade goes to the investment committee I already know that it's good because I've done detailed due diligence. Any trade that was bad or had a red flag has typically already been filtered out. However, this governance process is very important to share knowledge and stress test in a meeting environment. Everything has to be debated, even if I already know it's a trade worth doing. These discussions are a key layer of my due diligence process. And these meetings are fun. I know who's going to say no to what, and who's going to overcome that objection, and between us all hashing it out little details are resolved. We take detailed minutes of the meeting, and then the transaction is signed off pending final due diligence and satisfactory completion of a legal documentation process.

Step 7: Final due diligence

For the final piece of due diligence I do basic checks such as a CV check, a criminal check, ID verifications and Google searches and make sure the other party has never been bankrupt or held directorship of any bankrupted entities.

If the trade passes that last test, it's over to the transaction execution team to work through the legal documentation and negotiation process. Then it goes to the marketing and legal teams to prepare all the final details and marketing materials, which is a very rigorous process.

When the marketing and legal documentation for the investment is finalised, it's time to get started on aggregating investors.

Once we launch, the orders start coming through the platform and we begin collating investor interest. This post-launch period tends to spark a new wave of investor registrations as the word-of-mouth news about the new opportunity kicks in.

Advice for capital raisers

You'll notice that his book is investor focused. I'm including this section for those of you who might be in the business of raising capital.

Capital raising is hard. I have been on both sides of the coin my whole career, looking to raise capital and looking to deploy capital. It can be very time consuming for all parties. If you're looking to source capital through iPartners (or anyone else) here are a few tips and approaches I would use to position yourself with the best chance.

High level

There's no need to kill yourself on detail: at the first stage, simple dot points in an email can be enough for an initial scan. Just be very clear on the trade, tell them what you want and by when, the risks, the exit, use of funds, broad economics and the parties involved, including their experience. Our team at iPartners is very experienced and has seen a lot of transactions, so we will typically not need much of a back story — sometimes less is more. If initial emails are too long, it concerns me, as it can smell like overselling, which should not be required for a good investment. Try not to sell; just present the facts.

Initial call

Assuming you got through the first scan, this call is really a more detailed run-through of your dot points. This is a common-sense scan, testing your facts, understanding the personalities and gauging if you seem genuine and are on top of the detail.

Pitch book

After a teaser on the investment, and maybe an initial call to understand it, most investors will want to start seeing some detail. Enter the pitch book. Make sure it's pre-prepared. There's nothing worse than having a call with someone looking for capital, asking for a pitch book and hearing crickets for a few weeks. We would have already moved on to another trade by then. I recommend sending it within 24 hours.

Term sheet

We will form our own view on the terms and economics of the trade, but you should already know what you want. Put it into a one-to-two-page term sheet and send it with your pitch book. It can be rough and approximate, but at some point discussions will get to term sheet stage, so if you have drafted something, it may save someone some work and get things moving forward more quickly. (Strangely one of the hardest things at times is to actually work out what someone looking for capital actually wants: is it debt, equity or do they simply have no idea!)

Meeting

Be prepared. We would typically not sit through a page turn of a pitch book as it tends to be a waste of time. Maybe have two or three slides that tell the story and focus on those.

(continued)

Do some market research. I would prefer someone saying, 'No idea' or 'I will come back to you on that' than lie or spin around an answer. Spin is very easy to spot. Changing or twisting facts during a meeting is also frustrating as it tends to highlight a lack of preparation and winging it (though at times winging it is fine). You don't need to know everything, although most would expect you, as a minimum, to have nailed the facts in your own pitch book.

Negotiation

Be reasonable. It's a balance. If you want to grow, you need capital and investors need a return. Often, trying to get capital at the cheapest price can be a short-term play. What happens if you need more capital? A positive investor experience is the best way to secure medium- to long-term access to capital. I would look at a two-to-three-year play as a partnership and your capital requirements. Be less sensitive to price in the early years and look to drift pricing your way as you demonstrate growth in brand and performance, and as your choice of funding sources grow.

One last thing

Don't be intimidated or nervous. Most providers of capital will have quite a bit of empathy and are looking for partners. They have likely been in your position before in looking for capital. So relax, be yourself and tell your story.

Alternative asset classes

Part II

Chapter 4

Property

Most people would probably consider property the largest kind of alternative asset in Australia. There are several different property sectors, including residential, commercial, agricultural and industrial. Within those sectors there are three primary types of investment strategies that we will consider: property equity, property debt and property options. The most common are property equity and property debt.

Let's dive into these property sectors and types of investment strategies, starting with defining the property sectors.

Property sectors

The property asset class is a diverse one, attracting investors with varying degrees of expertise and risk appetites. It is a sector of the market where, as an investor, you need to do your research because you will be dealing with insiders (property developers/builders) with access to asymmetric information and capital raisers with conflicts of interests. This can lead to decision making that's not always in the best interests of the investor. Following is information on some property sectors to consider. The trick is to find a situation where the playing field is reasonably even.

Residential property

Residential property is anywhere that people live. It can be, for example, rural or suburban, a townhouse, an apartment, a low-rise or high-rise. Many people buy single residential investment properties, but in the context of investable alternative assets, the residential property sector tends to be residential development projects such as land subdivisions (e.g. dividing old farms into residential lots), townhouses, apartment blocks and residential towers.

Commercial property

Commercial property can be anything from an office space in a high-rise tower to the milk bar down the road. It can be a shopping centre or a childcare centre. It could even be a pub or a sports facility. There are many themes within the commercial sector. Golf courses, marinas and sporting grounds/clubs are examples of leisure commercial properties. Storage is another type of commercial property you can buy or develop.

I personally like commercial property where there is a positive carry (that is, an ongoing return over and above the interest and other costs of holding the asset). A positive carry for commercial property could be a land banking opportunity, which means a large piece of land that can generate attractive returns from a commercial activity such as storage facilities, industrial facilities, market gardens, turf farms or other agricultural ventures, and that also has the potential to be rezoned down the track.

Agricultural property

Strictly speaking, this is a subset of commercial property, but it's worth singling it out as it can be quite diverse. It can range from investing in the equity and ownership of a farm to providing a loan to a farmer to expand their land holdings, livestock and operations. We will look into agriculture in more detail in chapter 9.

Industrial property

Industrial property is another sub-class of commercial property. It includes large factories and warehouses used for purposes such as distribution, manufacturing, storage and production. These buildings tend to be on very large pieces of land that are great for industrial purposes and may also have the potential to be re-purposed or rezoned down the track.

Property equity

There are two main types of property equity: project-based property development and established assets, which are usually tenanted and largely de-risked.

Equity behaves a bit differently when it's in property from when it's in a business. For a development, you put your equity in, then 18 or so months later the project is finished (hopefully), the asset is sold to its end user and you are paid your equity back plus any return if the project was successful. If the project was not successful you may lose some or all of your equity (that's how equity rolls). By contrast, if you invest in the equity of established assets such as a fully leased office building, shopping centre or childcare centre, you are in it for the long game. Hopefully you will achieve some capital appreciation over time, but it tends to be more a rental yield play to compensate you for the risk, with more debt-like characteristics as it can be a reasonably stable capital value with consistent distributions.

Equity in development

Putting equity into a development is a bit like being an armchair developer (although in some projects where an investor would own a large percentage of a project, it can be a significantly more active approach — more like a back-seat driver!). You sit back while the developer does the work, with the key risk being driven by the success of the developer and the project. How good was their forecasting? Were there any cost blowouts? Was the work completed on time? Time can be a killer of equity returns on these projects because the longer you are funding the debt, the more it eats into the absolute equity returns as well as the relative return on a per annum basis.

An example is in residential land subdivision in a city fringe area that's transitioning from rural to suburban. Let's say a developer has received council approval to rezone a local farm to residential land. The developer wants to subdivide and develop that property, but they don't have enough equity in the project to satisfy a lender and source the debt to pay for all the civils (such as putting in piping and sewerage, roads and fencing) and development costs. They know (think) they are onto a good thing, so their solution is to take on an equity co-investor (you as the investor, or an aggregation of many small investors such as iPartners), who will share in the economics of the project as the developer has now sold down part of the project to you.

Equity in established assets

The other type of property equity is established assets. As mentioned, this could be a shopping centre, a childcare centre or any established business. You're buying the equity for potential upside in the value of the property and for the income it generates as an asset. In some respects, it's a bit like buying an investment property in the residential world. It generates regular income (rental yields tend to be higher in commercial and industrial property assets) that may go up over time.

In the commercial and industrial worlds there tends to be a positive carry on the assets, and banks generally offer a lower LVR, so they effectively won't lend as much against these assets. Often, a lead investor will need to raise additional equity so they can qualify for the bank's lower LVR and get the cheaper bank funding. This otherwise presents an investment opportunity for non-bank lenders to provide funding to developers looking for a higher LVR than that offered by the bank.

What is a non-bank lender?

A non-bank lender is anyone who lends money and is not a bank. Non-bank lenders are a big part of alternative assets, especially for property. The first port of call for most developers to get finance is the bank because banks have the lowest interest rates. Even though they're the least flexible, have the lowest LVRs and are the most awkward to deal with, their cheap interest rates make them the preferred option. However, there are many cases where a bank won't want to lend money, such as where a project is too small, the loan is needed quickly, the project is too leveraged (that is, the LVR is too high) or it's perceived as too risky or complex. This is when developers will look to non-bank lenders.

Say someone wants to buy a completed shopping centre in an outer suburb of Melbourne for $10 million. The bank agrees to loan them $5 million. The lead investor has $2.5 million, so they need another $2.5 million of equity. They might approach me to ask if I'm interested in putting in $2.5 million of equity (owning 50 per cent of the asset) because they might say that the property is going to generate 8 per cent income per annum and that they think it's going to go up over time. I would assess the investment and look closely at the operator's ability to manage and run the asset over time. I would also look at whether there are any value-add opportunities that could kick up the valuation or yield. (Yield is driven by actually being tenanted and properly maintained regularly.) If they could not source this equity (say I was not interested given the above analysis), they may try to find a non-bank lender prepared to lend $7.5 million and decide not to source the funding from the bank as initially planned.

Another version of equity in established assets is listed or unlisted property trusts. Although the term can mean lots of different things, it typically means some type of completed asset that is fully owned by a trust, has a moderate degree of leverage, generates a consistent yield and is paying a management fee to someone for arranging or running the investment.

What is leverage?

Leverage is a financial term that describes when an investor borrows money to invest. Borrowing money for a product amplifies your outcomes – both gains and losses. Let's say someone invests $100, but $50 of that is borrowed. When the asset goes down by 25 per cent they've actually lost 50 per cent of their capital. And obviously they'll have to pay back the debt at some point too. If you don't have a loan and the asset goes down by 25 per cent you only lose 25 per cent. So leveraging amplifies losses significantly. Many investors were caught out during the GFC by these types of products.

Twelve to 18 months is a typical length of time needed to complete these types of development projects, and investors can expect somewhere between a 20 per cent and 50 per cent return on capital. (Of course, it could end up being 0 per cent because development has risks. Nevertheless, land subdivision is probably my favourite sector for taking on development risk due to the relative simplicity of these projects.) It's potentially a pretty nice passive return on capital for the armchair co-investor, but it's risky simply because you actually own equity in the project.

Example of residential development land subdivision

iPartners co-invested into a residential project in an outer suburb of Sydney with a land subdivision property developer. The developer had a good project and needed someone to inject equity. We said we'd take 40 per cent of the project and put in $4 million. Our investors could put in anything from $10000 upwards, and we aggregated those 50-odd investors to generate the $4 million required to co-invest. So our investors effectively became armchair developers because the developer does all the work for a development management fee.

In situations like this we set up a project-specific company with the sole purpose of running the project, with 40 per cent

(continued)

ownership by the iPartners Project Unit Trust and 60 per cent by the developer. Then that project company takes on the property construction (contracting various parties to complete the works). This involves getting all the council approvals and contracting to put in the infrastructure, such as roads, power and pipes. We are not actually building anything on the land because the land will be sold to individuals or families to build a house, or to a builder to build a few houses. In many respects these are the simplest projects because we don't actually build the physical property, although we do take on the complexity of dealing with local councils, which is arguably the toughest task of all.

Let's look at some types of risk involved in property equity transactions.

Risk in property equity transactions

Staying with residential land subdivision projects as an example — though the logic also holds for other projects — if property prices fall by 20 or 30 per cent and you are trying to sell your freshly subdivided residential lots, you could either sell them at a lower price than you originally expected, which eats away at your equity returns, or hold onto them for longer, which eats away at the equity returns through funding interest on debt. As with any equity investment, you could lose money.

As far as capital structures go, equity is the riskiest part of the project. A return of anywhere between 0 and 50 per cent is commensurate with the risk.

The difference between 0 and 50 per cent is usually due to the financial forecast not being accurate, extra costs, weather, regulatory issues or the project running overtime. The local government might introduce requirements for additional approvals you did not expect (or missed), additional geologist testing or soil testing, or it might ask for things that you weren't expecting. It might rain for six months and you can't get on site. It's all the uncertain variables that drive the difference in returns and risk. This is why due diligence on the developer is critical before investing. How many projects have they completed? How strong is their balance sheet? How have their previous projects performed relative to forecast? And, crucially, what skin do they have in the project — that is, how much will they lose if the project goes bad? The higher the number, the greater the project alignment.

If you are lucky enough to take on one of these projects in the environment when property prices are going up, you can get returns that are quite attractive and outsized from the forecast. You'd benefit from the developer's profit margin and property prices going up while the project is on.

If you then get your model forecast correct and finish on time, it can be quite nice. Finishing on time is important because it avoids blowouts in interest payments on the money you borrow for the project. Imagine you have an 18-month project and you borrow 60 to 70 per cent of the cost. This means you pay 18 months of interest. If the project ends up taking two and a half years, that's an extra year of interest you have to pay, which will eat into your equity returns. A project taking longer than projected is an important risk to be aware of.

For the Sydney project mentioned earlier, the returns were at the lower end of the range because selling off the last few blocks was slow due to increased supply in the area. It took longer than forecast, so we ended up carrying those assets and the associated interest costs longer than we needed to. That's the reality of it. If we had cleared those assets more quickly, we would have had returns at the upper end of the range. That's equity. Be ready to tolerate some volatility and uncertainty or don't buy into equity risk.

What is volatility?

Volatility is best thought of as a proxy for the risk of an investment. If the price of your investment moves around a lot in a period of time it has high volatility and if the price is quite stable in the same period it has low volatility. There are more complex explanations on the mathematics of the calculation and how it can be used in option pricing and other forms of modelling, although for our purposes, this book uses it as a risk measure.

Property equity aggregation strategies

Aggregation strategies usually start with a small portfolio of property equity assets (often the physical asset and the operating company stapled together) that is progressively built up to be an institutional size portfolio that can be sold to a large fund manager or progressed to an IPO (initial public offering). The most common in recent times are associated with pubs and hotels, although they are increasingly becoming more prevalent in the agricultural space as well.

Example of co-investing in rural pubs

iPartners co-invested in some rural pubs after a couple of blokes who owned three country pubs demonstrated a good track record of turning them around into successful businesses. They were starting to tap out of capital (both their own and the bank's) so after completing very detailed due diligence on the project, we went down the now well-trodden path of aggregating small investors to a larger size and co-invested into this initially small fund alongside the founders.

The fund adds new pubs every few months. We now own a few in Wagga Wagga and Albury among other rural locations. Our investors are armchair owners of country pubs. It's the regular purchase of additional pubs that created the equity aggregation strategy and our investors actually own small pieces of each pub and its operations. They own the real asset: both the pub's property and the operating business.

The fund borrows about 50 per cent of the money from the bank at a relatively attractive rate. This leads to an attractive expected return per annum of 15 to 18 per cent, which is a combination of potential equity accretion (the pub land values go up) and income, which is the return from the pub's operations.

This is how it will grow to be a big fund. Assume they find a new pub to add to the portfolio. The pub costs $20 million. The bank says it will lend them an additional $10 million against the asset of the pub but they will need $10 million of equity. If we liked the strategy, we (iPartners) would put in $2.5 million of equity and they or their other investors would contribute $7.5 million. So we effectively contribute 25 per cent of the required capital. This new pub gets added to all the other pubs in the fund. This exercise is repeated over and over until the fund is large enough to achieve an exit for the investors.

We got in at time zero, when they added their first pub to the original three. The fund has about $200 million worth of pubs at the time of writing and there are another few in the pipeline. This suggests the exit is getting closer than we first thought it would, as the fund is now approaching a size that will be attractive to an IPO or sell as a package to a larger institutional investor.

Pubs are expensive, although they can be cash cows. If you buy into the right areas, they can also be land banks: they go up in value as urban creep encroaches on regional land. They can be a nice asset class and our investors are getting this access.

I quite like aggregation strategies because you can invest more over time as you start seeing success (or stop investing or invest less if you do not see the progression of expected performance) and the investment progressively becomes de-risked as your investment ends up being spread across multiple assets.

Property REITS

A property REIT is simply a listed fund of property assets. They became increasingly popular in the 2000s. Many would include these in the alternatives bucket, and they can be an okay set-and-forget investment. They are a more liquid way to quickly get property exposure, but they also tend to be quite correlated to traditional equity markets, primarily because they are listed and when investors get bullish or run for the gate, all listed assets can behave in a correlated manner. This higher level of liquidity on the listed market can add additional price volatility to your asset.

Property options

Another key way to invest is through a property option.

What is an option?

Options can be applied across many types of investments and assets. Put simply, an option is a contract between two parties that gives the buyer the right—but not the obligation—to buy or sell an underlying asset at a predetermined price at a specified time in the future. This means you can 'lock in' an optional buy or sell price for, say, three months' time, giving you price certainty. No matter what it is actually worth at that time, you have the option to buy or sell it at your previously agreed price. Of course, if the price of the asset has gone down you probably won't choose to action your option to buy. You'll let it go and forfeit the price (option premium) you paid for the option. But if the price of the asset goes up, you get to buy it for a discount, which makes the option premium you paid for this option very worthwhile!

Let's say you have a piece of rural land in your sights right next to land that's been rezoned from rural to residential. You've formed the view that the council will potentially rezone this land and convert it to medium density residential or industrial or any form of rezoning that may lead to an increase in valuation.

You go to the person who currently owns the land — you can knock on their door or get an agent to do it — and say, 'Will you sell me a call option on your land today?' That means, as the investor, you will pay them an option premium today. You might agree on a three-year option giving you the right to buy the land at any point in the next three years for, say, $25 million.

You might give them $1 million (4 per cent) cash today for that call option. The option will only be exercised if the value of the land is greater than the strike price of the option. (The strike price is the price the owner agreed to.)

So, if you pay $1 million today, you have the option — but no obligation — to buy the land for $25 million at any point in the next three years. The current owner then has to sell it to you at that price because it's a binding contract between two parties.

If the value of the property does not increase, you've lost your $1 million. The minute you pay the premium, that money is gone. You can potentially sell the option to a third party before expiry, so you might be able to sell that option during the three-year period to someone else who sees value in it. But if it gets to maturity and the property is worth less than $25 million (and you're not buying it) you've lost your money.

Leverage in property options

The key thing with options is the enormous leverage that's factored into them. If I pay $1 million for an option on a $25 million property, in a way I have 25 times that leverage. What this means is that I paid $1 million for potential exposure to an asset worth $25 million. So if that asset grows in value to $31 million, I'll exercise the option and buy it for $25 million (ignoring stamp duty for simplicity, although in reality it would need to be considered). Just imagine I then sold it for $31 million! The first million was the option premium because I don't get that back. So the effective cost base is $26 million ($25 million + $1 million). I sell it for $31 million, so I've made $5 million before tax. A $1 million commitment gave me a 500 per cent return on my capital!

Option leverage is great once you get above the breakeven point. In options, breakeven is the point at which the asset price appreciation equals the amount of premium you paid.

So the minute the asset goes to $26 million, you've made back the million you paid in premium. After that you can high-five yourself because you have an awesome leveraged return. If the value goes from $26 million to $27 million, you have a 100 per cent return on your money even though the asset only went from $25 to $27 million. The asset is only up by 8 per cent, but you achieved a 100 per cent return because your equity was only $1 million at the start and you had enormous leverage.

The downside is that if the asset stays at $25 million, or drops to $23 million or $24 million, that money is gone. Options are awesome on the upside, when they work. They're also not bad on the downside because your downside is truncated — in this example, the maximum you could lose is the $1 million option you put down.

It's quite common for people to take an option on large rural plots of land on the edge of urban creep or targeting any rezoning opportunities. The seller may not expect the value to go above $25 million so they think it's free money — until it gets exercised. Then, when it gets to, say, $31 million, they may feel it's a bad trade. That's property options.

Example of a property option

iPartners recently had the choice of onselling an option. There was another year or so for it to run. It was coming through the COVID-19 era and we decided to onsell it. It wasn't worth the risk of holding as we could redeploy capital. We didn't really want to be involved in the project. So we sold the option. We received back 100 per cent of our premium and a small return as we had bought well. If the risk-return equation or macro

(continued)

environment starts skewing against you and there is an exit opportunity, usually the best choice is to hit it and move on to the next investment.

The group who bought it from us was a large property developer. They thought they could make more money out of it through exercising the option and completing the project. They thought they'd be more advanced in a year and could exercise the option, then move on, whereas we got to the point where we'd had enough of being involved in it and were ready to move on to something else. It was a rational rather than an emotional assessment. That's the way these things can go. You get a range of outcomes on investments like this one.

Property debt

The third strategy is property debt (although in reality there are all sorts of combinations and permutations of the three strategies). Investing in property debt has become very common in private markets. It has become so mainstream and so commoditised that you could even argue that it's no longer an alternative asset.

As a result, at the time of writing I've been struggling to find value in investing in property debt for a while. The market is very saturated with promoters of property debt investments (when things change, so will my view!). I don't mind it from a risk perspective. I think that in the property space, structured correctly with the right LVR, you can find quite a nice asset from a risk perspective.

What I don't like is the return side, when an asset class is quite saturated with a supply of cheap capital, with a lot of lenders going after the market. Because there are a lot of lenders, it means an excess supply of capital goes into that market.

An excess supply of capital means the borrower can get cheaper interest rates, which is great for the borrower. It's basic economics: the supply-and-demand equation (excess of capital) is in the developer's favour, which simply means the relative return on me investing in property debt isn't there.

From my perspective, I care about my investors. I want them to maximise the return that they get for a given risk. The risk-return equation for debt is heavily skewed in the borrower's favour at the time of writing, whereas I prefer things to be skewed in the investor's favour.

Having said that, it's still a relevant strategy, and as I said, things change, so let's take a look at the various types of debt instruments and how they can work when things change again.

Capital structure

The first thing to get your head around is the concept of capital structure — also referred to as capital stack. We touched on capital structure in chapter 2. We are going to take a deeper dive here.

Figure 4.1 (overleaf) highlights the fundamental risk-return overview of investing in property debt. The lowest risk debt (lowest return) is at the top of the capital stack. This is the senior secured loan and is the first to get repaid and the last to lose money. The loan types below this increase in risk and return the further down the stack they are, with the highest risk debt (highest return debt) being the last to get repaid and the first to lose money after equity.

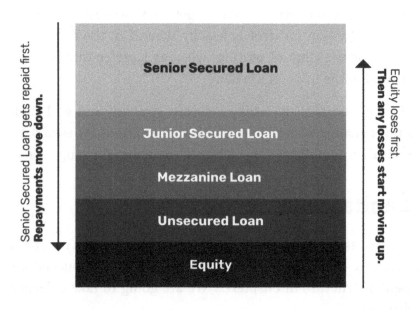

Figure 4.1 Capital structure

Not all these levels are used in every property transaction. The structure could be as simple as including only equity and a stretch senior secured loan (sometimes the word 'stretch' is added to indicate there is no junior, mezzanine or unsecured loan — that is, the senior secured loan starts at the bottom of the stack and stretches to the top). This is the simplest of capital structures and my preferred one because having fewer parties involved means less time is spent on legals, and they can be easier to unwind or restructure if things go wrong.

Senior secured loans (first mortgages)

The investment opportunities in this area tend to vary widely although the most common tend to be development loans, land bank loans and high LVR loans. It's an area where the banks — the cheapest lenders — don't typically want to play, primarily because they tend to be considered more complex projects or loans. Banks tend to play in the more mature, later stage and completed assets.

DEVELOPMENT LOANS

For ease of explanation of a senior secured loan (which can also be called a first-ranking registered mortgage) let's go back to our land subdivision and look at a development loan. The borrower bought the land, and they own it. They now want to pay for all the contractors to come in and do the construction and they need to borrow some money. The logical source of funds for them (assuming they cannot get bank funding) is a loan from an investor on a senior secured basis. The loan should be documented by the investor as first ranking, senior debt and a mortgage placed on the land registered with the Registry Office and likely a charge over the borrowing company or trust registered on the PPSR (Personal Property Securities Register). If you register it as a senior secured loan, first ranking charge, then it's recorded as being the security. *Note:* before you ever lend money, you should run a PPSR and title search to ensure no other party has recorded an earlier charge on the company or specific assets. If they have, ensure it is removed before proceeding with any new debt facility.

First ranking security (senior secured lender) is important because it means all of the assets of the project are pledged as security to the investor, so if things go bad the senior lender is repaid first. This means if the borrower goes into default and can't pay interest or repay the loan, the asset will be sold to repay the loan and the senior lender is the first to be repaid. The repayment includes interest and penalty interest (penalty interest is basically a higher interest rate that is charged if the borrower is in default or in breach under the loan terms). After the senior lender has repaid other creditors, more junior lenders can put their hands up for repayment. Being senior secured is obviously less risky than investing in the equity, but you've still got development exposure.

The nature of construction debt is that it tends to be drawn down over time. Think of it as a bit like a line of credit. For example, if a developer borrows $5 million to finish the development, they might draw down $500 000 a month across the duration of 10 months. That money is in a land sub division project used to put in all the infrastructure such as roads and sewers, and the developer will pay interest on that loan. The interest is paid in two ways: as a line fee on undrawn money — meaning an interest component is payable on the full amount of debt even though they haven't drawn it down yet — and on drawn funds. The interest on undrawn money tends to be a lower rate of 1 to

2 per cent, and the interest on drawn funds is higher. The total interest payable is a combination of the undrawn and the drawn interest amounts. They'll typically pay an application fee too.

Example of a progressive project debt drawdown structure on a development loan

iPartners loaned $20 million to a developer for a land subdivision project on a senior secured basis using a progressive drawdown structure. The purchase of the land was funded by the developer's equity and we agreed to progressively lend up to 70 per cent of the asset's value. The developer then dug the roads and did some construction works – which added value to the asset – and got a new valuation. When we received the new valuation to validate the increase in the asset's value, we authorised the next drawdown and loaned them more money. In this case the value added in the first phase of the development was $5 million. We loaned them $3.5 million (70 per cent LVR – that is, 70 per cent of the $5m increase in value) for the next drawdown.

This process continued throughout the project. The developer did the work and got a valuation, and we continually loaned them money at each stage of the work. We didn't give the developer $20 million upfront because they would then have been receiving money without the project improving (so in a fire sale the asset value would unlikely have been high enough to repay the loan and the LVR would have been greater than 70 per cent). We only lend on increased asset value once the work is complete. And we only care about the value today because that's the amount we can use to get our money back. A theoretical future value is no use to us today.

That loan paid just over 12 per cent per annum (plus a line fee) across 18 months. It was quite a nice asset.

The way most of these construction loans work is that you factor the interest cost (as there is no project income to pay interest until it is complete) into the total repayment amount. You can do this in two ways: on maturity or upfront.

Interest on a loan like this is often payable on maturity (aka capitalisation). If you think of a home loan, you probably pay principal and interest every month. However, here all the interest is paid at once at the end because the developer doesn't have money to pay until they progressively sell the vacant blocks or start generating income at the end.

Say, for example, we lend a developer $30 million, which they draw down over time. When it gets to maturity, they owe us $30 million plus compounded interest for the 18-month period of the loan. From a lender's perspective you simply factor that into your model: 'We've loaned $30 million, and our risk is actually $30 million plus interest. We're effectively lending, say, $32 million. We consider this a $32 million risk.' Even though the notional loan is $30 million, they owe us $2 million in interest at the end. You just factor that into your model when you're calculating the LVR.

The other way of doing it is that you effectively factor the interest into the progressive draws in the project. The project pays the interest periodically, and you're really getting paid your own money back along the way. Economically it's the same thing. The reason you would do it this way is because the investors might want to be paid interest monthly, which means the developer needs to pay interest monthly. It's a bit circular because the loan actually goes up. You're just lending an amount upfront that funds the interest across the term. In many respects it's really a marketing twist.

In this example, you are loaning them $2 million additional at time zero (so it's still a total loan of $32m like the one above). That $2 million will be used to pay the interest on the loan along the way. You get to the end and they only owe you $30 million (because you received the interest along the way). It's purely mathematical. When it comes to repayment of principal it's the same whether they pay you interest in the end or along the way.

LAND BANKS

Another common form of senior secured debt is over land banks (large pieces of vacant land) and pre-development sites. These assets are pretty much parking bays for developers and property owners. They either think the property value will go up over time or will be rezoned, or they need time to get development applications in place. Banks generally don't like financing these types of assets as they usually have no income of note to pay the interest on the loan, although they tend to have relatively low LVRs. The interest payments are typically made from the owner's other funds or capitalised and paid as part of a refinance at the end of the investment. They can be reasonably secure investments from a risk perspective due to the low LVRs and significant excess security. The main risk due to the typically low LVRs tends to be refinance risk because that's ultimately your exit.

HIGH LVR LOANS

In a senior secured loan, the LVR tends to drift between 50 per cent and 75 per cent. With 75 per cent, you know that the 25 per cent below you is the net equity component and possibly junior debt, which either way is someone else's problem in a default situation. Say the value of the project is $10 million: if you've done a 75 per cent LVR first ranking registered mortgage you know you're lending $7.5 million against the valuation of the asset. That's senior secured.

There can be high LVR senior secured loans (again, banks typically won't touch them), which are often used as bridge facilities. 'Bridge', in this context, means a short-term fix until an owner can rearrange their finances through an asset sale, capital improvements or in some other way. These loans can be risky due to the lower security coverage, although they tend to come with a story: 'Jimmy is waiting for another property to settle, then he will refinance with a bank'; 'Jenny had an overrun on another development so she needs to borrow more against this asset to finish that project.' However you look at the scenario, the owner has stretched themselves. If this is temporary and the exit makes sense, maybe it's a worthwhile investment, although whenever the asset coverage is lower (high LVR) and the owner is stretched through mismanagement or excessive risk taking, it's typically a red flag to dig deeper in your due diligence, walk away, or ensure you are getting paid a high interest rate to compensate for the risk.

Note: every time I talk about a 'higher LVR', it typically means you're getting paid more interest (because you're taking on greater risk). There's a continuum. When you get down to a second mortgage, unsecured or caveat loans with high LVR, you can be getting paid as high as 18 to 25 per cent per annum, if not more, because you're getting into pretty edgy risk.

Junior secured loans

This investment is again an income-producing debt where you share the security with the senior secured loan. The key difference is that you are second in line for repayment — although you still have the benefit of being part of the first mortgage registered security — so you are second behind the senior lender. Often, this level of debt won't exist in the capital stack and you'll simply have the two or three levels: the senior lender (first mortgage), mezzanine debt (second mortgage) and equity, although I've included this for completeness.

Let's say you have a property project that needs $30 million to happen and a senior lender says, 'I'll give you $17 million of debt if you put in $13 million.' You only have $10 million of equity, which equals $27 million, so you are $3 million short to complete the project and keep the bank happy. One way to cover that is to get a junior secured loan for $3 million (if the senior lender consents to sharing the security on that basis).

It behaves pretty much just like the senior loan, but tends to be drawn down first. That happens because the senior secured lender says, 'I'm not lending you a dollar until there's enough subordination in there, or enough protection, which means I want to see $13 million in there before I lend' (your $10 million and the $3 million junior loan). This means the junior loan of $3 million gets drawn down first, and might pay for the first road to be built or the first drain to be put in. Once the junior loan has been drawn down, the senior lender says, 'Okay, this is fine. The value of the asset and contributed capital now makes sense. I'm prepared to come in and lend the remaining $17 million.'

So it behaves similarly to the senior loan, but it ranks behind the senior one in the repayment waterfall. A repayment waterfall is the order in which creditors are repaid if there is an insolvency or exit situation. In our example, the senior lender is paid first, the junior lender is paid second and the owner (or the equity holder) is paid last (if there's anything left over).

From the junior lender's perspective, if there are losses on the project, the junior lender will lose money after the owner, but before the senior lender.

Example of a junior secured loan

We became the junior lender on a build-to-rent project. This is when a developer is building a reasonable number of units, not to sell, but to own and rent. We provided a junior loan to fill the gap between the equity and senior debt. We aggregated investors and loaned money to the developer. We ranked behind the senior lender. We typically don't really like doing junior loans. The only reason we did this one was because it had a 60 per cent LVR. This meant that even though it was a junior loan, the leverage ratio was still quite low. We thought it was a really nice risk even though we ranked junior from a security perspective.

We got all our interest paid and we got our money back. The coupon (interest) was at about 11 per cent per annum, so it was a nice return. It was also only a 15-month project, so it was pretty quick. It was a nice little trade. When we're looking for trades, it's always about the risk-return. Even though we don't like being junior in the capital structure, if we are junior and the return on risk is still attractive, we will consider it.

Mezzanine loans

The next level below senior and junior secured loans is mezzanine loans. The terminology here can be confusing for investors because capital raisers use different descriptions for slightly different security arrangements — for example, mezzanine loan, second mortgage, caveat loans. I tend to bucket them all together from a risk perspective as 'mezzanine finance'.

Basically, mezzanine finance is where you register a second mortgage (a bit like a junior secured loan but documented differently) or you have a caveat, which is a right to register a second mortgage on the project. You don't get the first ranking security on the asset because it's already been taken by whoever gave them the first mortgage. As a mezzanine financier you only have security after the lenders who have the first mortgage.

The risk assessment for mezzanine investing involves closer scrutiny of the LVR and who is the senior lender because you might conclude it's still a good trade basis. You may be ranked behind a bank with a conservative LVR, so you are providing the top-up debt piece, often at attractive pricing, which may make sense. A mezzanine loan below a non-bank lender can make me nervous at times as I will wonder why they are not doing the loan themselves. This is just a red flag — not a 'no'. Make sure you do the due diligence.

Unsecured loans

The final loan type is outright unsecured debt. This is where you're just sort of hoping you get your money back. You form a view on the sponsor and the developer and you form a view on the project, cash flows and LVR. But you've literally got no security or any right to register security. I call them 'hope loans'. We tend not to do them at iPartners, but they do exist and people do them.

I'm not really sure why people go into hope loans regularly. I think it's greed, and possibly asset allocation. If you're someone extremely wealthy and you see a little hope loan that's paying 25 per cent, you might put $10000 in it. There's a certain amount of money where people think, 'Well, who cares?' So, in asset allocation it can be about the money that you're happy to completely risk. For really wealthy people, $10 000 is the equivalent of putting $50 on a horse. They don't associate it with gambling, but really that's what it is. It's an amount of money where people don't really care about the risk-return because they have invested in all sorts of other things that might work, and they can afford to lose $10 000.

You might have an investor who says, 'I'll invest 95 per cent of my money in senior secured loans, with low LVR positions earning 8 per cent. I might then invest 5 per cent of my money in hope loans earning 25 per cent. On a portfolio basis I'm not really taking that much risk.' Or maybe the investor knows the sponsor really well and thinks, 'I've known this person for years. It feels like equity risk, but I've been investing with them for years, and I'm going to back them personally to get this right.'

We won't do these trades often (if at all) because of our fiduciary role for investors. We need to represent our investors' best interests and it's not worth the risk of doing that sort of trade when it's got such an uncertain outcome. When we can do other investments with a better and more attractive risk-return, we prefer to focus on those.

Low interest rates and property debt

Even though at the time of writing we are in an interest-rate hiking cycle, on a relative basis interest rates are still low, so investors have been looking for assets with higher yields. At the same time there have been a lot of new funders of property assets raising capital from investors. Once the capital is raised by funders, it needs to be deployed or it will be a drag on investors' expected returns. This has led to an excess of capital ready to be deployed to developers. The risk and return goes in cycles, but as it sits now, I can't see it changing in the short term. Property debt investing doesn't look great in value due to the saturation of money ready to be deployed to the asset class. I prefer to invest where there is a scarcity of capital.

The barriers to becoming a property lender are quite low. What I mean is this: if a valuer says a piece of land is worth $1 million, you might say, 'Well, I don't think it's going to fall too far in value, but to be safe, I'll only lend 60c to the dollar.' You can then go to any legal firm and they'll give you an off-the-shelf document to allow someone to sign up to a senior secured loan investment, and then another document to register a mortgage on the property for the benefit of investors. Then you register it. And you're done — you've become a property lender. This means there's an excess of people prepared to provide capital in that market because it's all pretty simple, low/no barriers to entry. The ease of entry into this market is contributing to the excess supply and making the equation look better for the equity owner than investors because they can source cheaper debt.

Weighing up risk and return

At iPartners we look beyond the limited metrics of traditional lenders. Sometimes we do smaller trades if they look like they will lead to bigger ones; sometimes we can see the risk is less than the banks think it is.

There was a particular developer who had a good bit of money coming in 12 months' time. They had quite a few assets, but the banks wouldn't touch them because they didn't have enough income. We looked at them and thought the developer actually had a lot of asset coverage across his portfolio. It was clearly a short-term window during which he didn't have the income, but we knew he would in a short period of time. So we said to him, 'We'll lend you the money for 12 months and we'll take these other completed residential property assets as security. You can pay us 11 per cent for the year.'

He knew it was the only way he could get finance and that we are easy to work with. It was a small amount and only for 12 months and he was keen to get finance on this asset. We were prepared to provide it and we understood the risk was actually a lot lower than the banks would have thought.

The property was worth around $3.5 million with a 70 per cent LVR on a stand-alone basis. We're happy to do smaller trades. The other good thing about smaller trades is that you learn from them. The smaller trades also tend to lead to larger ones. This particular person was a large and experienced property developer, and doing that trade ultimately led to our involvement in another of his nearly completed projects.

We actually had equity in the developer's other project and understood the asset well. We knew it was worth roughly $15 million. The size of the $2.45 million loan ($3.5 million × 70 per cent LVR = $2.45 million) was very small relative to the size of the project, the broader asset pool and the expected windfall. We'd already factored in the project going wrong, or taking longer than expected, or property markets crashing. We factored in all the possible bad scenarios, and we still could have been repaid three or four times our money. You just have to think mathematically, and analyse the worst-case scenario. It's not necessarily how traditional lenders think because they can be very regular-cash-flow focused.

I like complex trades and security that are hard to understand. This is because there's a scarcity of capital where things get hard. Banks and larger non-bank lenders like things easy and repeatable, so if it's complex, they will say no. Other lenders won't be able to understand it and they'll say 'too hard' or they don't know how to solve the problem. Whereas I'll look at it and think, 'This is brilliant! I'm going to be the only lender here. I can structure this deal. I can reduce the risk by having security and different levels of protection and I get paid a premium return for it.' There aren't many people getting paid a premium return for a simple 70 per cent LVR single property residential mortgage (with substantial other security temporarily locked up). Because we were prepared, on behalf of our investors, to quickly consider the complexity of the security and solve for it, we got this great return.

It's literally where there's a scarcity of capital and knowledge, that's where the value is for investors. If it was easy, everyone would be doing it.

That's why senior secured property lending is saturated — because it's easy. That's why there's an excess of capital there and the returns are not that attractive. It's a genuine alternative asset, but it's an easy one.

I really look at risk and return. I have a database approaching 15000 investors. With that many investors you have a whole sweep of society. You've got a self-funded retiree who just wants their money back with a little bit of return to give them a bit of income every month. Then you've got a 28-year-old aspirational lawyer or banker who wants to double their money. The risk-return profiles of the investors are broad.

If I look at an asset that's paying 5 per cent when it should actually only be paying 1 per cent, I say, 'That looks like a pretty good trade.' If I can negotiate a 5 per cent return on something that should only pay 1 per cent, I'm going to go to my investors and say, 'Well — risk-return — if you can get this asset at 5 per cent instead of leaving money sitting in cash or doing nothing, it looks like a pretty good relative value trade.'

I care more about risk and return than I do about absolute return. If someone offers to pay you 20 per cent, that's a massive number. If you then realise they're putting all your money on red at the casino, that's a bad trade. For the money on red you want to be getting a significantly higher expected return (in reality on red or black it's always a bad trade, however you look at it, because the probability of a win is statistically less than 50 per cent).

It's the risk-return that has relevance. I want to get paid a greater return for the relevant risk.

Return-wise in alternative assets I wouldn't be targeting anything below 6 per cent (at the time of writing, risk-free interest rates are currently trending up. This number needs to also trend up to retain the private markets premium that I am looking for). This is mainly because you are typically taking on an illiquid asset and there needs to be a premium for that risk. I normally try to target high single-digit returns or double-digit returns — something greater than 10 per cent. I think it's about greater return for a given risk. We partially get that from simply scarcity of capital, illiquidity premium and complexity premium, among other risks. Where there aren't many people playing, it's an intelligent sort of premium.

Chapter 5

Equity

When it comes to making alternative investments in equity, it's helpful to think about it in two ways: the stage of the company you're investing in, and the type of equity capital that you will hold. We have touched on property equity already, although we will dig into it a bit more deeply and broadly in this chapter. Let's start by looking at various stages of equity capital sourcing.

Equity capital sourcing

The stages of equity capital sourcing differ depending on who you speak to, although I think of them as angel, seed, growth capital (for simplicity, I have bucketed this with venture capital — strictly venture capital tends to be a bit earlier stage than growth capital), debt with warrants (not actually equity but it can be part of the equation), pre-IPO equity, traditional private equity and anywhere in between.

Angel stage

Angel investing could be the result of a couple of people who turn up with an idea and a PowerPoint presentation. They say, 'We're pretty smart and we reckon this is a great business idea. This is why we think it's great and this is our story. We don't really know if it's going to be successful or not, but we're prepared to have a go. Can you give us some money?'

That's it! Just a wish and a dream. But they've got a pretty slick PowerPoint presentation. The business doesn't actually exist (yet), but it's a nice story. We're often not talking huge sums here. They could be trying to raise $10000 to $100000 to start work on their proof of concept. That's angel investing.

The things that matter for an investor at this stage (aside from being prepared to lose all your money and/or dip into your pocket regularly to provide more capital) are the individuals' backgrounds. If you are going to believe their dream, ideally it's in a sector they have some experience in. Have they started businesses before? Were they successful or close to successful? There is experience in failing, so a previous fail is not necessarily a bad thing (it's not good either) — it's a learning lesson. How much are they risking? Have they left a high-paying job, and invested their personal capital and time, or is this a hobby on the side? What do they stand to lose personally if they don't succeed. Other investment advice books probably won't ask this, but I would also ask if they have played sport, music or had hobbies and been successful? Have they succeeded academically? I personally like to see a track record of success or attempted success so I can assess whether they will push hard to succeed or vanish at the first sight of a late night. It's a very qualitative assessment.

Seed stage

Seed investing is the next part of the journey. They've taken that PowerPoint presentation and built that first widget. Maybe it's a tech business with an app in development. At this point the app doesn't actually work but you can click the buttons and it shows the journey of how the consumer experience may work. They've invested the time and effort and there are a few dedicated people involved, probably a couple of full-time staff or founders, who aren't earning much money because they're trying to live out their dream.

They're trying to raise some money — more this time, maybe $500 000 to $1 million — to take their rough design to the point where it's potentially commercial. In the case of an app, this would mean developing the app to user-testing phase, or maybe even to a beta version that can generate some revenue.

By the end of the seed phase, if they've survived and developed a potentially viable product, they start looking for larger chunks of growth capital, where they are ready to commercialise their product and get it out there to their target market. This is when larger, proper investors start coming.

The capital raised in the angel and seed phases is typically raised through personal savings, friends and family, or crowd funding. Once people get into the growth phase they will be looking for their first real investors — that is, people who genuinely believe their story.

The assessment for whether to invest is quite similar to angel investing, although it's slightly less of a throw of the dart because the concept is now touchable, close to real. They have probably worked out what they are doing, have a PowerPoint presentation on steroids and are getting good at pitching the story for capital.

My thoughts on angel and seed capital

I personally don't like direct investing at the angel and seed capital stages. They are a bit like hope loans. The range of potential outcomes is simply too wide, the risk is too great and the required due diligence significant. You could either make an enormous amount of money or lose all your money. There are lots of losers and not many winners in this space so it's quite risky.

If you are interested in this space, I would recommend investing with specialised fund managers who are building out a diversified portfolio of assets, or restricting yourself to sectors of the market where you have personal experience and knowledge — for example, for me, it would be finance, funding, investment, platforms and related industries.

Growth/venture capital stage

When it is ready for growth capital (also overlapping with the venture capital phase), a company has already achieved proof of concept and has an okay business, or it has a reasonable business and is heading towards profitability. It's building its reputation in its segment and starting to perform. It's possibly already got a brand name and may even have a venture capital or growth fund investor on its register, which could give it some credibility.

Growth capital is sort of an interim step. It's where businesses have spent a lot of their capital, have likely invested significant sweat capital and simply need more to grow. They may have spent their initial round of capital (from the angel and seed stages) and be only halfway through building their tech platform (for example). Their consumers have said, 'I love it', but they need to add features A, B, C and D and they need to hire a bigger tech team, so they need to raise more capital, typically at a higher company valuation. Every step of raising capital for the business should see (ideally) upward revaluations of how much the business is worth.

These businesses will be looking for equity, usually in the range of $3 million to $10 million — maybe more. I tend to get approached at this stage, and usually there is a lead investor, which could be a venture capital fund, who says, 'We're putting in $5 million. Would you be interested in putting in $2 million to wrap up the round?'

At iPartners, we've done growth capital investments with finance companies and platforms that have the potential to achieve significant scale through technology applied to really profitable businesses. All of these investments are similar in that they need some equity to bridge them so they can invest in more technology or services and grow their business. We're prepared to invest because we can see the potential for really attractive returns at some point in time.

Example of growth capital investment

In recent years, we've seen quite a bit of growth in non-bank finance providers. These are new ventures that, for example, offer home improvement loans to consumers so they don't have to go to the banks to borrow money. The product is all about convenience, with borrowers able to source loans right

(continued)

at the point of sale from retailers on larger items, such as a new pool, roof, blinds and other traditional consumer items. They are designed to be scalable platforms largely driven by a scalable tech offering and a broad universe of supportive retailers offering the service.

They can be fast-growing businesses. We have invested on a co-investment basis with other large investors in this area. We target expected returns of 50 per cent to 150 per cent for equity because it's all about risk and return, and we are taking a larger risk due to the earlier stage investment and the less predictable investment outcome, although we have seen enough of a path to be comfortable selectively in this category.

Debt plus warrants

Debt isn't actually equity but can be part of the equation. I'd like to talk about debt for a moment because there's potentially a debt step involved at this stage. Once companies get to the growth capital stage, they can either source more equity, or if they've got money coming in and are profitable, they can potentially take out a loan (debt). This type of debt may include some equity warrants (think of these warrants as a call option on the business given to the debt investors — so debt plus warrant investors will share in some of the upside of the business through owning the warrants) to be less dilutive even with the warrants to shareholders than issuing new equity (dilution is when the existing shareholders' ownership percentage of a company decreases as a result of the company issuing new equity). This is technically a part of private credit (private credit is explained in the next chapter). So it could be a funding strategy of some new equity plus a new debt capital injection.

Let's say a company is doing well and starting to generate some positive EBIT (earnings before interest and taxes), basically making a profit. The directors of that business will say, 'Should we raise growth capital now and dilute ourselves and other shareholders? Or would someone give us some debt?' Deciding to borrow money instead of issuing equity leverages the business up and increases risk because it's a drag on cash flow, but the shareholder is often quite happy because they get the capital without diluting their slice of the pie.

Not everyone can get debt though. They need to have certain characteristics. There needs to be some form of asset or cash flow that can be used as security (like a receivable or asset pool), or give the borrower comfort on repayment. (A receivable is simply money owed. It tends to be money owed by a customer for the provision of a good or service to them by a company. Since the company should get the money at some point, it is an asset that can be used as security.) If there's no asset and no cash flow, it's often very hard to get access to debt (I wouldn't lend in this instance). If that's the case, they will have to issue equity in this growth capital phase to get the money they need for growth.

As a company grows, they reach a point where they can choose whether to issue equity or take debt. Their access to finance significantly increases because they have choices. That's the overlap between the private equity type markets and the private credit markets.

Pre-IPO stage

This is the nearly grown-up phase. Business is chugging along and the founders think there could be an exit coming, but the business needs some capital to accelerate into an IPO (initial public offering).

Growth stage in pre-IPO — a cautionary tale

In the broker world, the description 'pre-IPO round' is excessively overused and at times misleading as sales spin. Technically, all companies that have not gone to IPO are pre-IPO. However, in the market it's generally accepted that pre-IPO means an investor should expect an exit via an IPO in one to two years. You need to be careful though, because some capital raisers will use the term to suggest the maturity will be shorter and that there will be a potential uplift in price. On investigation the reality could be that there is almost no probability the company is going to IPO in the next three to five years, let alone one to two, so it's not really a pre-IPO round. It's probably at growth capital stage. At times I have even been shown what looks like seed capital called a pre-IPO raise.

Okay, back to the facts. 'IPO' is the term used to describe a company about to list on a stock exchange. When companies decide to list on a stock exchange, they usually like to really accelerate their growth into that listing, which often requires a bit of capital, so they'll call it a pre-IPO funding round, with the capital largely deployed for growth. In theory this is the last capital raise before listing.

All the rounds discussed previously tend to be straight equity (other than the debt + warrants bit that snuck in) — that is, you're typically getting real equity in a business. While pre-IPO rounds can start to look a bit equity- and debt-like in nature, they're often convertible structures. Convertible structures are discussed in more detail under the heading 'Types of equity capital', but there are different kinds. For example, they can be a SAFE note (simple agreement for equity), which typically pays no coupon (interest) and which offers you a discount into the company's equity if they do an IPO or a more traditional convertible.

There's another, more traditional convertible structure that will pay a coupon of say 8 to 12 per cent per annum. If the company goes to IPO, you will get into the company at a discount to the IPO price. Discounts can range from 10 to 30 per cent. The best way to think about it is, say you buy pre-IPO convertible notes and pay $100. If the company goes to IPO and you had an agreement to get a 25 per cent discount, and the company's IPO is $100 million, you're effectively buying equity at 75 per cent of that value as you get a 25 per cent discount with the maturing proceeds of your convertible, which converts to equity at the point of the IPO (sometimes you will be given the choice to take cash).

Obviously that's pre-IPO. The whole journey up until listing is in the alternative asset class because it's hard to access without an investment platform and all of these forms of capital live in the private markets world. Once listed, the equity is in the public markets and quite freely available through traditional online brokers, so it's no longer an alternative. There was a trend to list some private credit funds, which would loosely fit in the alternatives bucket, although they have tended to trade at significant discounts to NAVs (net asset values), so at the time of writing that market feels a bit slow to near dead, at least in the short term.

Growth capital and pre-IPO equity stage

I think growth capital and pre-IPO are quite attractive investment opportunities because you can see a more predictable path and distribution of potential outcomes and exits. I've also started seeing some interesting co-investors and funds entering at this phase. Knowing that the big guys are playing and we are providing access for our investors alongside them can provide some comfort. Although this interest is rising from institutional players, there's still a scarcity of capital because there's less expertise in understanding real businesses and therefore fewer people are interested in investing at these stages. For this reason, this is my preferred bucket of equity.

And there's an alignment of interest because you're typically backing the key founders, who are still running the business and are keen for the last sprint to exit and for their, and in turn their investors', payday to arrive.

Example of investing a pre-IPO

I was approached by a workforce services company for some equity-like funding to accelerate growth into a potential IPO in the next 12 to 18 months. The solution offered was a convertible note, which paid a 10 per cent per annum coupon and had a discount entry price into the IPO at 20 per cent below the price (the convertible was preferred over equity for the coupon, but also because it was difficult to get comfortable with a straight equity valuation).

This is hybrid in nature as it has both fixed-income and equity characteristics. The fixed income is the 10 per cent per annum on the loan, and the equity side is the option to buy equity at a 20 per cent discount when the company lists. This discount means for $100 in the convertible, you would effectively get $125 of value. So, assuming the IPO price was $1, your $100 ($100 divided by $0.80) = $125 of value in the IPO shares.

This hybrid structure can be a win-win for both parties. The existing equity holders like this because it delays and reduces the dilution of their equity as they are not issuing straight equity at an earlier stage with likely a lower valuation, and investors are happy as they are being paid a high yield and will get a discount if all goes to plan.

Of course there's a risk that the IPO never happens, or that the company underperforms and there are delays in the return of capital, or worst-case scenario, loss of some or all capital. These are equity-like risks, so the trade ranks in capital structure below senior and junior debt, but typically above equity.

Private equity stage

Taken literally, this could be defined as any equity in a private company, although the term 'private equity' typically refers to a stage of the investing cycle. It tends to be quite a strategic stage where a reasonable-sized investment is made by the private equity firm. The investment usually comes with some control from both an equity ownership percentage and through seats on the board — as well as, most likely, some other investment rights — and often funds a partial or full exit by founders. The goal of private equity is typically to get in, influence, add some value, then achieve an exit of multiple times your money in three to five years.

I like private equity, although it can be a hard one for investors because there's usually a very large cheque required. You will often be investing alongside or in a large private equity fund, which gives some comfort, but also some loss of control.

Types of equity capital

The different types of equity capital you can invest in are straight equity, preferred equity, deferred equity, convertibles/hybrids and equity options. Various blends of their characteristics are possible although for simplicity I have attempted to bucket them. Let's dive in.

Straight equity

Straight equity is the simplest of trades. It's when you buy equity in a private company (you own part of the company). This is typical for the early investment rounds in companies. Angel, seed and even a lot of growth capital investments are straight equity as it's the only form of capital really available to the company at this stage. Straight equity is calculated on a predetermined valuation of the company's worth at the time you make the investment. There is no maturity, and your investment exists in perpetuity until the company doesn't exist, or is sold, or there is a liquidity event and you can sell your shares.

This is the riskiest bucket of equity capital (options are probably riskier, but they aren't strictly equity — they are equity-like).

Example of a straight equity investment

iPartners provided debt financing to a company in the property management and finance sector that lends money to property owners, secured by future rental streams. So, if you own an investment property and expect to get $10000 in rent for the next 12 months, the company will lend you the $10000 now, and when the rent comes in, they'll take the rent money to get paid back. And, of course, there's a difference in the amount they pay property owners upfront and the rent they will collect over the 12 months, which is called 'factoring' or 'discounting', and there's an interest rate element as well.

Initially iPartners provided the company a great big loan and took security over their finance company. The company then provided lots of little loans with the money we loaned them. It was an asset-backed debt relationship.

Then the company said, 'Look, we want to grow faster. And to do that, we need more equity in the business', which meant they wanted to sell part of their company so that they could get extra money into the business and use that money for growth. A large venture capital fund decided to invest the majority of the capital raise into the company. But they needed additional equity capital to round out the raise, so they came to us for the difference. We liked that there was a large reputable venture capital fund leading the round; it was good validation of our already positive view of the company. We knew the company really well because we had provided them the debt funding. We did our own analysis and decided, 'Yep, this looks like a pretty good trade. We want to own part of this company.' That's effectively what equity is: you literally own part of the business.

LISTED (SECONDARY) VS UNLISTED (PRIMARY) STRAIGHT EQUITY

When you buy equity on the stock exchange, you're effectively buying equity in the secondary market because you're buying it from another investor. Because the company has already raised the equity in the past (equity exists in perpetuity unless equity is bought back or is in wind-up), it's secondary market equity.

In the example above it's in the private market — that is, unlisted. We were buying the equity directly from the company and owning part of that business. It's primary market equity because it's the primary creation of new equity. (To confuse things, if I then sold it to someone else after the primary creation, that would be a secondary sale of the equity in the private markets.)

In the private market equity there's more risk. Unlike fixed interest (loan/debt/credit), where you get a quarterly coupon and you get your money back at the end, with equity there are no guarantees. You're taking the view that this company is going to go well, even though the outcome is uncertain. But the returns can be much higher than for something like fixed income. If the company doubles in value, you double your equity value. With straight equity investments in the private market you would typically expect a return that is multiples of your investment. With the straight equity example above, we're expecting to get three to four times our money back over a three-to-five-year time frame. That's a pretty cool return (when it works). But there's risk in a potential return like that. There's a chance you'll get back nothing. That's what equity risk is. You own part of a company, and if it does well, you win. If it doesn't do well, then you lose. It's an area of investing with more uncertain returns.

Preferred equity

Preferred equity is when you invest in a company without actually owning any of the company directly in return. Why would anyone do this? Because it has a more defined return (if things go well) than straight equity.

Preferred equity has equity-like downside, meaning if the company bombs and the straight equity investors lose money, typically the preferred equity investors will also lose some money. But crucially, preferred equity is ranked senior to straight equity, which means straight equity will lose money first, before preferred equity loses money.

Where preferred equity really differs from straight equity is on the upside. You tend to get a preferred return before equity does. Let's say you get to maturity or an exit with a preferred equity investment and the company has made $100. The preferred equity investors might get the first $25, and the actual equity owner gets $75. Where it becomes really relevant is say the company only makes $25. Then the preferred equity investors will get $25, and the equity investors get nothing. As a preferred equity investor, you're getting your money first.

When investing in a company, the equity holders typically get the highest return when things work out well. But when things go bad, equity gets the worst return. And preferred equity just means you get a preferred return before equity holders get it.

You can be preferred in a liquidation event as well. Say a company falls over and the assets recovered amount to $80. If the senior debt was $60, the preferred equity was $20. Then the senior lender and the preferred equity would be repaid in full, whereas the equity would get nothing because there's nothing left over. In this situation preferred equity was preferred in distributions and return of capital.

WHY DO EQUITY HOLDERS ALLOW PREFERRED EQUITY?

Equity holders tend to be optimistic (especially founder equity holders). They think everything is going to go well, which is why they take on the greatest risk. And when someone invests via preferred equity rather than straight equity, they like it because it doesn't dilute their ownership.

Say someone owns 100 per cent of a company, and they sell me half of their company as straight equity to raise funds to grow the company. I get half of the upside if things go well. That's great for me, but they've lost half their company. In contrast, if they offer me preferred equity, they continue to own 100 per cent of the company, and they just need to give me a preferred return across the investment term. It could look like a 25 per cent return and a share of the profits at the end or along the way.

So the benefit to the equity holders is that it doesn't dilute them. And if you own part (or all) of a company, you don't want to be diluted because that reduces your upside. One of the ways not to dilute yourself is to issue preferred equity: you're giving someone else the preferred return while keeping 100 per cent of the equity upside.

Preferred equity is a tweak on the standard straight equity risk-return profile.

Example of preferred equity

I use a lot of property investment examples in this book as they tend to be simple, although the basic logic can apply across various asset classes. A great example of a preferred equity trade is one iPartners recently put together for a land subdivision in north-west Victoria, just outside of Melbourne. Our investors purchased preferred equity units in a trust that will rank senior to current equity holders and subordinate to senior debtholders. The preferred return for this is 15 per cent plus a percentage share in the project profits. It is estimated that the completion of the development will be achieved in 18 to 24 months.

Originally when this opportunity came our way we were going to put in straight equity. We told the developer, 'We'll put in $5 million and we want you to put in $5 million of new equity. That way we rank exactly the same. We'll go into this deal as a partnership.' This was important to us so that we knew our interests would be aligned. But the developer didn't want to match our $5 million equity because he had already put in money at the start of the project. He owned 100 per cent of the project at this stage, and he needed capital to continue it.

We said, 'That doesn't work for us because we're relying on you, as the developer, to do this project well, so we want our interest to be perfectly aligned with yours. If you're not prepared to put in more money, then we want a preferred equity position, so that we rank above you. We want to get the first return on all of our investment before you get a cent on your original equity.'

He was happy with this, and we made it a preferred equity investment with a few investor-beneficial twists. We wanted alignment of interest, and by being senior to him on the

(continued)

return profile we were creating that. We rank in front of him and will get our principal and returns first, while he is still motivated to maximise his return on his equity, which in effect means that he's protecting iPartners' interests. That's why a preferred equity trade was the solution. It's all about alignment of interest and structuring the deal in the best way for investors.

Deferred equity

Deferred equity is not a typical investment instrument; rather it tends to be used with staff or advisers as a way to pay them for their services. I decided to include it in the book because I get asked about it at times.

Let's say I have this cool new business and I want you to come and work for me. Based on the role and your skills and experience you should be paid $250 000 a year. But my business is not making enough money so I instead offer to pay you $100 000 each year, and in two years' time I'll give you 5 per cent of the company. That 5 per cent is deferred equity. I'm acknowledging I can't pay you what you're worth, but I really want you to work for the business, so we sort of go into business together. If it works out, you'll own 5 per cent of the business, which will hopefully be worth a lot more than the $300 000 of lost income over the two years. You're also highly incentivised to help the business soar because you know the better it does, the better you do. You're going to have equity in the business, but you're not getting it until you put in two years of service. So you take personal risk on your income for potentially a huge upside.

It could be the same with an adviser. Let's say a company isn't profitable, but could be doing really well after overcoming a few hurdles. An adviser might say, 'Well, I know you can't pay me today, but I think your business is going to be worth a lot of money down the track. So I'll provide my services, and in two years' time I want 10 per cent equity in the company.' This is deferred equity — you can think of it as deferred payments or deferred compensation. With deferred equity there's always a condition required for you to get the equity at that later date. It's very similar to staff incentive equity options, which we discuss next.

Equity options: time, price and other triggers

I have included this section on equity options because there are various derivative strategies utilising options and volatility strategies that many would bucket into alternative assets. It can get a bit complicated though.

As a quick reminder, an option is a contract between two parties that gives the buyer the right — but not the obligation — to buy or sell an asset at a predetermined price at a specified time in the future. The option to buy under these circumstances is referred to as a 'call option', and the option to sell is a 'put option'.

There are a number of types of options in the equity space. There are staff incentive equity options, which are often issued for free or at a low strike price, creating alignment of interest between the company and the staff. This is very similar to deferred equity, but with deferred equity staff get the equity, whereas an option gives staff the right (but not the obligation) to buy equity. And there are also over-the-counter options and exchange traded options.

As the name suggests, exchange traded options trade on the stock exchange. Over-the-counter options are an agreement between an investor and a counterparty (they are not listed on a stock exchange).

Let's start by looking at an example of an exchange traded call option as an easier starting point.

As mentioned, a call option gives you the right (but not the obligation) to buy an equity at a certain strike price at a certain time. For example, I may buy a call option to have the right to buy BHP shares at $100 in three months' time. And say in three months BHP is trading at $200, I'll absolutely buy it for $100. So I've pretty much doubled my money (in reality I have made significantly more on a percentage basis as I would have only risked the option premium to enter the position). But in three months if BHP shares are trading at $50, I definitely wouldn't buy the shares for $100, so I'll just burn the premium I paid for the call option.

Over-the-counter options on listed equities work the same way, but they are a bi-lateral contract between an investor and a counterparty. The key here is the extra risk. Often the counterparty is a bank, which reduces the risk. Banks are highly rated entities: they're regulated, and they have capital, so the counterparty risk with them is quite low. But if it is a random seller down the street without capital backing them, the risk is high because they might take your premium and never give you the benefit. You need to consider counterparty risk with over-the-counter options, whereas if you do it listed on the stock exchange, the counterparty risk is largely removed by the exchange through the requirement to post margin. (Post margin means the option seller needs to send some cash to the exchange upfront — and maybe more on an ongoing basis — which sits there as security to ensure you get paid if a trade works out in your favour.)

Call options are often used by investors, and put options are often thought of as insurance for an investment, although traders can use them to just take a leveraged trading view either way.

With the BHP example, let's say it's trading at $100 and I buy a put option giving me the right to sell you BHP shares at $100. Three months later BHP is trading at $200. I'm not going to exercise my put option because I want to sell the shares for $200. So I let that option expire: it's worthless, and I lose the premium I paid for the put option upfront. But if after three months BHP was trading at $50, I'd be over the moon that I bought the put option as insurance. I'd exercise my put option, selling you BHP at $100 even though they're currently trading at $50. A put option is a way to insure another position, or if you have the contrarian view that an asset price might fall, you can buy it purely as an investment as well. (*Note:* you don't have to actually buy or sell the shares. You can often cash settle rather than physically settle.)

You can trade call or put options without owning the shares themselves, doing it as a leveraged trade to try to make money. If you buy an option (pay premium) you could have the view that it will go up and you will sell the option and receive back more premium than you paid, or hold it until maturity and hope it is in the money. ('In the money' means the actual share price is above or below — depending on the option — your exercise price. In my example above, the BHP put option is in the money if BHP is trading at $50 and you can exercise the put and sell your BHP shares for $100.)

Now, to complicate things a bit, you can also sell options outright (not owning any position in the underlying equity). If I decide to sell the put option, and get paid a premium for it. I'd be selling that put option to someone who has the opposite view — they think it's going to go down and are looking for insurance on the share. If I had sold that put option and then if the equity value fell (the view was wrong), I would potentially lose a chunk of money because I have to pay out the sold put option if the buyer exercises their option. But if the equity value goes up, they won't enact the put option and I've made money from the premium.

The price of the premiums for options are driven by the volatility in the market, the interest rates in the market and the expected forward price, with the asset price move often the biggest factor in the price of the premium over time.

HOW DO OPTIONS RELATE TO COMPANIES AT THE DIFFERENT STAGES?

In the early stages (angel, seed, growth capital, pre-IPO), you tend to either buy equity or you don't buy equity, and you source debt or you don't. In the later stages of a company, where you can have people with opposing views, the potential is opened up for equity options to occur. An investor could take a call option on later-stage equity (call options are very popular in the property acquisition space), or they could take a put option on later-stage equity with the challenge being finding a counterparty to take the opposite side of that position. So one party might think a specific company is going to double in value in the next year, and another thinks it's going to zero.

They have a totally divergent view, and then can meet in the middle and say, 'If you think it's going to double, then I'll sell you a call option and you pay me 10 per cent today. And if the company doubles, you're going to get a nice payout from it. But if the company goes to zero, I've made 10 per cent upfront from the premium.' However, finding someone with an opposing view from yours can be hard in the private market, which is why it's usually done over the counter (bi-lateral contracts) and often among founders, staff or associated entities not as exchange traded options (obviously because the companies are not listed).

Most options tend to be covered positions (that is, there is an underlying equivalent ownership in the equity of the same company referenced in the option contract, which is different from a 'naked position', where there is no ownership of the underlying equity). So, for example, an owner of 100 shares of private Company Z is happy to give an investor a call option on, say, 50 shares at $10 in the next 12 months. The buyer says, 'Fine I think the next raise will be higher. I will pay you $1 per share today as premium.' The buyer, though, says, 'I am concerned you might sell these shares.' They then come to an agreement that the buyer can register a first ranking charge on PPSR over the seller's shares in Private Company Z as well as signing up to a bi-lateral option agreement. The buyer now has some security, the seller gets their premium and now they wait! These kinds of agreements can also occur between founders and staff members where shares are illiquid and views on exit timing and personal life get in the way.

Options for other assets

Jumping outside of equities for a moment, you can buy a call option on any sort of underlying asset in any asset class.

It could be corn. It could be sugar. You could buy a call option for sugar for its current price because you think it's going to go up 200 per cent. That's an investment in an alternative asset: it's a different way to take exposure to sugar. In chapter 6, I explain structured products and futures, which are also derivative in nature. The key difference is that with futures each party is obligated to buy or sell, whereas with options the holder has the right, but not the obligation, to buy or sell.

Convertible bonds and hybrid securities

Firstly, the terms 'convertible bonds' and 'hybrid securities' are often used interchangeably. (They are technically different, although there are so many permutations of both that it's easier just to bundle them together and read the documents for the specifics if you are ever looking at investing.) They have the same characteristics as a debt instrument in that they pay interest, and they also have characteristics of equity instruments (and tend to be unsecured or deeply subordinated), plus the option to convert debt into equity if an event such as an IPO occurs. I touched on this earlier in the chapter, but let's dig a little deeper.

Say I have this cool company and I don't want to sell you any of it because I think it's going to be worth multi-millions. But I definitely need money from you because I need money to grow. That's when the option of a convertible bond comes in. I would say, 'I don't want to do equity, and I don't really want to do preferred equity. Can I make it more debt-like and just pay the investor a fixed-income return? That's better for me because it's less dilutive.' The potential investor might be thinking, 'Actually, I wouldn't mind having some upside in this company. So how do I get a little bit of upside with it looking like a bond so I get some compensation across the journey?' Enter convertible notes. These are usually done in the private equity, growth or pre-IPO stage, particularly as early days companies don't have the revenue to pay the total interest, so offering some equity upside potentially compensates the investor for the lower interest amount they receive relative to the risk.

Convertible notes look like a fixed-income investment in that you have a fixed maturity (which adds refinance risk to the company if you have not been converted by the maturity date as the maturity may be quite a bit longer than stated), and you usually get paid a reasonably high coupon (interest rate). You get a high coupon with convertible bonds because the downside is equity-like and unsecured, meaning if the company underperforms, you've typically got absolutely no security whatsoever because you're close to the bottom of the capital structure. So when things are going well it behaves like debt because at maturity, if the company's performing well, you'll get your money back. You'll also have received a nice coupon — say 10 per cent per annum — paid every quarter over the time frame. But when things go badly with the company, the risk is equity-like — that is, you can lose your money alongside other equity holders. And that's where you get this hybrid nature of a little bit equity, a little bit debt.

The slight twist with convertible bonds is that you have an option that gives you the right to convert to equity upon some events occurring. So rather than reaching maturity and getting your money back, under certain circumstances you can choose (or be forced) to convert your money to equity, usually at a nicely discounted price, which is the reason investors consider it, despite the heavy risk.

Let's say there's a convertible bond that gives you the right to buy equity at a 20 per cent discount if the company IPOes (lists on the stock exchange). Investors will think, 'Well, this is pretty cool. I'm getting paid 10 per cent per annum, and if this company does list on the ASX (Australian Stock Exchange) for say $100, I can buy them for $80 because I've taken this risk on the company before they've IPOed.' That's the convertible element: the right to convert into equity at a discount upon certain events.

It's hybrid-like because it behaves like a bond in a perfect world, where you just get your money back and a nice coupon along the way. It's equity-like because if it goes bad, you're going to lose some or all of your money just like you would with equity. And it's a convertible because at some point, you can convert your debt-like instrument into real equity at a discount if there's an IPO.

This is why people call these 'hybrid securities'. There are many different variations of how you can do them, but this is the standard approach.

SAFE notes (simple agreements for future equity)

A SAFE note is a simple agreement for future equity. I find SAFE notes tend to get offered when a company is performing well or has a strong story and plenty of investors are keen to invest. This means the company can drive the terms. Usually when investing in a company, whether it's straight equity or a convertible note, I find the company needs the investment; therefore the investor has the power to negotiate some terms. With SAFE notes, the company doesn't want to sell their equity cheaply because they think it's going to be worth billions, but they need money to grow, so they offer investors SAFE notes. SAFE notes are becoming increasingly popular in companies that have a strong growth story. Company founders are effectively offering exposure to their company by issuing a SAFE note and you might get a discount entry into the company down the track.

Investors pay them money, receive no coupon payments and don't get their money back at a fixed point in time (if at all). They sit and wait for an exit event. What investors get is equity-like downside and the right to convert to equity at a discount if an event occurs. The only benefit for investors is getting into the company at a discount at a future point in time. But between now and then, they'll get no return on their money. They're *very* favourable to the company owner as they're non-dilutive upfront and less of a cash drag on company capital.

The redeeming feature of SAFE notes is the valuation cap. A valuation cap means upon conversion to an equity event, the valuation used for the conversion is the lower of the current capital raise valuation and the valuation cap. As an example, if the company valuation at the time of conversion was $100 million and the valuation cap was $50 million, the SAFE note owners would get roughly twice as many shares upon conversion because they are effectively buying shares at a $50 million valuation, whereas the company valuation is $100 million.

SAFE notes are rarely favourable enough for me. I typically push back on the structure as I have a preference for straight equity or a traditional convertible. I'll only consider talking to someone about providing capital if the risk-return is fair to slightly skewed in my favour. I'll offer alternatively doing a convertible bond or even straight equity, but if they're fixed on wanting it to be a SAFE note structured in a favourable way to existing shareholders, I would typically walk away unless there is an amazingly compelling story.

Walking away is a great investment strategy. Not doing a trade might not make you money, but it can save you money, and saving money is always better than losing money.

As many old, important, grey-haired people say, 'The investment I did not do was one of my best.'

Chapter 6

Credit

Private credit is the investing space where senior secured debt, junior secured debt, asset-backed lending, structured and project finance, mezzanine debt and other forms of unsecured debt happen and exist across a wide range of underlying asset classes.

A lot of the time you can get attractive returns in private markets through simply providing the capital quickly, while banks and large institutions can be difficult and slow to work with. It can take three months to get approved for a loan from a bank. On the other hand, private markets can approve a loan within days or weeks.

Given that businesses often only need funding for a short period of time, they are often happy to pay an interest rate that's 3 per cent or 5 per cent higher than the bank's because they want the funding right away. They want to get on with running the business and expect to make so much money from it that they can afford the higher interest rate. You often get paid for convenience in the private markets.

Note: parts of this chapter overlap with sections in chapter 4 because debt can be applied to different asset classes. This chapter has more of a generic approach than chapter 4, which is specifically on property.

Senior secured loans

Say you have a company that's looking to borrow $10 million to grow the business, and they've got absolutely no debt in the business. You would typically first look at doing a senior secured loan (sometimes called a corporate loan if lending to an operating business), which is ranked the highest in the capital structure (capital structure is explained in chapter 4).

As a reminder, a senior secured loan is the lowest risk form of debt from an investor's perspective. 'Secured' means the loan has security attached to it, which means if something goes wrong the person who loaned the money has a claim against an asset to recoup their money. (Be mildly careful of a senior secured loan to businesses that have no tangible assets because in this instance you don't really have security, even if it is senior secured. Review the historic financials and balance sheet). 'Senior' means you are ranked the highest, so if something goes wrong you are the first to receive money in any wind-up event. You also tend to get paid the lowest return if there are other more junior forms of debt in the capital stack.

Typically in a senior secured situation, your security is over that company and all its assets, and is registered first on the PPSR.

To explain this simply, think of how in the residential property world the bank that gives you a mortgage for your house has a senior secured position against your home. So if you don't pay your interest or repay your loan, the bank will take your house to sell it so they can make their money back. A senior secured loan in the private credit space is very similar. You're investing money and taking security over the company. So if the company doesn't pay the interest or pay back your money, you could force the company into default and attempt to sell any assets to recoup your loan. (The key difference in assessing a property loan versus a corporate loan is that for a corporate loan the focus is on cash flows and profitability, whereas in property the main focus is the LVR.)

For an investor, a senior secured loan can be a pretty boring investment: you invest the money and you typically receive monthly or quarterly coupons (interest) and your money back on maturity, just like lots of other fixed-interest instruments. Boring or not, there's still a risk that it might not go well, so you will want to ensure that it is well documented, your charge is registered on the PPSR, and the value of any tangible security that can be sold for the recovery of your investment in the worst-case scenario is enough to cover the loan repayment and the interest.

In the corporate lending space there's less capital available (as in asset-backed lending) because it can be complex to analyse. The investor needs to analyse a balance sheet — that is, analyse an operating business. Although it tends to not be as attractive as asset-backed lending due to the idiosyncratic nature of the risk of lending to a single company (which is discussed further below), the scarcity of capital available for corporate debt still makes it an interesting space to generate attractive investment returns.

Example of a senior secured loan

An energy company was purchasing another energy company and doing an equity raise to fund the purchase. They also required some debt. The metrics of the transaction (the speed of their requirement for funding and complexity) didn't lend itself nicely to bank finance because banks take a long time to approve loans. So we provided a senior loan to this company where we were earning 14 per cent per annum on a three-year loan that started amortising after 18 months. (This means some of the principal started getting paid back, through quarterly distributions, at the 18-month mark.)

It was a scarcity-of-capital transaction. Not many other lenders were considering the asset because it was a bit complex. The company needed a senior loan to buy the energy company and we were prepared to fund it. I liked the asset because it had quite strong EBIT (earnings before interest and taxes). There was strong profitability, very experienced management in that sector and a very large pool of receivables on the balance sheet.

Receivables are an asset that gives me extra comfort.

Energy companies get energy at wholesale. Then households and retailers use that energy and pay the bill. Households paying a bill is a receivable, and there are lots of households who have bills to pay, creating lots of receivables.

Therefore receivables become an asset on the borrower's balance sheets. If the company falls over, we can potentially benefit from the collection on the receivables (the security) as the bills are paid—because, as investors, we want our money back.

At the same time as us doing the loan, there was also an equity injection, and the equity was subordinate to our position. A lot of that equity injection came from management, which meant the alignment of interests was really attractive. Management was buying in on a personal level. The CEO was taking money out of his own pocket to buy more shares in his own company. That equity, in conjunction with the debt we provided, was used to purchase the new entity. That's the best way to summarise private credit, or a corporate loan.

This loan was refinanced in full after about two and a half years with a full repayment of principal and interest to investors, so it was a good experience in hindsight.

My natural preference is not to over-invest in this space, or at least to minimise my exposure to it. The reason for that is the idiosyncratic risk of single companies. If I've got $100 to lend, and I lend $100 to one company, 100 per cent of my capital is exposed to that company.

If they underperform or there's fraud or a disaster of some kind, then all my capital is exposed. But in certain situations it does make complete sense. Sometimes it could be a diversified business with lots of assets as receivables on its balance sheet or other security, which reduces the risk. Then I'll get comfortable. But my preference is to not be overexposed to corporate loans in a diversified portfolio.

Junior loans

As a company grows, if they already have a senior secured loan in place and they want access to more debt (rather than issuing equity and diluting shareholders), and if the senior lender says, 'I'm not lending you any more money because I don't think your business is quite up to it', they've got to look elsewhere. This is where they will look for an investor that is prepared to provide some debt funding on a less secured basis, such as a second ranking charge on the company. As the name suggests, these investors are second in line behind the senior lender in the event of any problems with the company, which means they would expect to earn a higher coupon for taking on higher risk than the senior lender. Although, as above, in a perfect world it would be another boring fixed-income return and their money back when all plays out as expected.

Unsecured loans

This is where we fall right to the bottom of the capital stack, just above equity, and are starting to swing in the wind on the risk-return spectrum. It's best highlighted with an example.

Say I have JettGusBuddy Pty Ltd, and the bank has already done a senior secured loan and subsequently put in place a first ranking charge (security) on top of my business. The bank now has control and I can't do anything about it if I want another loan. My only choice is to go to the bank and ask for more money, or I could refinance the bank away and put someone else in (hopefully getting the larger loan I want). If I don't want to take either of those two options, I might just go to someone and say, 'Will you give me an unsecured loan on this, for these purposes?' Who knows? They just might.

This is where unsecured debt comes in (it has many different names). Unsecured debt is riskier for the investor, and because of this, the borrower usually pays a higher interest rate on this kind of loan because it has no security. The investor can only expect a positive outcome through the business generating enough cash flow to fund the interest and repay the loan over time.

The current senior lender (the bank in this example) has the company and all its assets as security, and now an unsecured lender comes along and says, 'I'll lend you money because I think you're a good business. I can see you're profitable. I'm okay with your profits and I think you'll be able to pay my principal and interest back over time. So I'm happy to do this without security.' JettGusBuddy Pty Ltd likes this person as they have provided the capital for growth without the business needing to re-engage with the bank.

As an investor, I would think very hard before offering unsecured debt. If I did, I would ensure I invest a small amount at a very high interest rate.

Unsecured debt is risky ...

I rarely invest in unsecured debt because I like control when I invest and when someone else controls the security in front of me, I have no control. In fact, at the time of writing we haven't done one unsecured debt trade at iPartners (though I have invested in some in my personal capacity outside of iPartners. One was paying 23 per cent per annum for a six-month investment, as an example).

Where it does possibly make sense can be when the senior lender is a bank and says, 'We'll give $10 million to the borrower over $20 million of assets, but we're not prepared to give you more than $10 million and we are not prepared to allow another lender to register a second charge.' If the company needs a total of $12 million, they might approach investors in the private credit space saying they want to borrow $2 million more. Let's say they approach me, and I go through their balance sheet and like what I see. I'll say, 'I'd be happy to lend $2 million.' I know the bank is conservative and won't give up any security because they're the senior lender, but I'm still happy to give the $2 million loan because I look at the serviceability of it and the assets on the balance sheet, and I see these guys can clearly afford it. The only reason they're not getting more senior debt is because the banks are being conservative and are subsequently refusing to lend any more, likely due to internal restrictions.

That is a situation where it could make sense to do unsecured debt. Although you lack legal security through registered charge (that is, security registered on the PPSR), you have practical security, even though this is not registered, and protection because the business has excess assets and cash flow, providing structural protection. This would be more than enough to get a full return of capital.

BRIDGING FINANCE

Another circumstance where unsecured debt can make sense is as bridging finance. Bridge financing is when you 'bridge' a short-term funding requirement for a corporate entity. It could be that someone is purchasing or about to purchase a new business, and they need some capital for a short period of time. You might do bridging finance unsecured because it's a highly profitable business and it's only for a short amount of time. In this circumstance the company would approach the private credit market (rather than the banks) for the loan because they couldn't be bothered dealing with the banks (plus banks take much longer to approve a loan). If you want finance quickly you go to the private markets. They'll assess the opportunity and decide, 'This is a good risk. They want money for six months. I expect their profits and a re-refinance will repay this loan in that time. I'm just providing a financing facility for a short period of time.'

Bridging finance can be secured or unsecured. If it's unsecured it's typically due to someone else having already locked up the security. Once the security is registered with the PPSR register, it's done. There's no more first ranking security left to give out for a later loan and you will rank second unless the first charge is released.

DEBT PLUS WARRANTS

When a business is relatively early-stage — say, in the seed or growth capital phase — and looking to put in place a senior secured loan as they are approaching profitability, the investor may consider that they require additional compensation for the risk to provide a loan, or maybe the company can't afford to fund the high interest rate that would match out against the risk-return view from the lender. In this situation, the company could add warrants (think call options) to the loan agreement. This means the investor who provides the senior secured loan will receive options, which typically exist for a fixed period of time (not always), that give the lender the right — but not the obligation — to receive straight equity in the company upon exercising the warrants. This is the kicker that gets the lender comfortable that they are getting appropriately compensated for the risk as they will potentially own part of the company in perpetuity, and if the company is successful the return could be significant for investors.

Asset-backed lending

Asset-backed lending is the asset class I like the most from within the credit space because you have a real asset (typically a portfolio of assets) sitting behind it. Typically you'll have control of that asset if things go wrong. An asset-backed loan is at its best when you are lending to a segregated company (this will typically be called a 'SPV' — Special Purpose Vehicle — in documentation, which will be a stand-alone company or trust) that holds all of the assets but does not have the operating costs of a business, because it can be a more controlled and predictable outcome for investors.

Let's look at a hypothetical example: Mr Big Car. This finance company has a wholly owned company called Mr Big Car Lending, which takes down a single large loan (borrows) from, say, iPartners (as illustrated in figure 6.1). Its only activity and use of those funds in the daily business is to lend money and earn interest. Say they lend money to lots of people to buy cars and Mr Big Car Lending takes all the cars as security (asset backed by cars). They've done 100 car loans of $1000 each. So there are 100 people who borrowed $1000 to buy a car. The security on that $1000 loan is a car and there is also full recourse to whoever borrowed that $1000. The benefit of having 100 loans is that even if three of these people don't repay, that's only 3 per cent of the portfolio.

The risk for investors is greatly diluted by lending small amounts to lots of borrowers, and there are assets sitting behind the loan that you have claims to. This is the true benefit of asset-backed lending over a portfolio of assets: your single investment is diversified across lots of small loans.

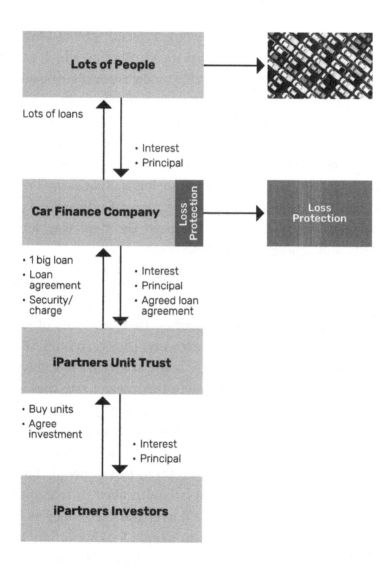

Figure 6.1 Asset-backed lending to a segregated company

The investor protection on the large loan provided by iPartners is further enhanced because we would expect Mr Big Car Lending to provide equity subordination (loss protection) so that they would lose money first. So, in the example above, the 3 per cent loss in the portfolio would typically not be a loss for investors. It would be a small loss for Mr Big Car, which would largely be offset by the profits they make from their business. By contrast, if you lend $1 million to a company and they go broke, you can lose the whole $1 million. In the example of 100 people borrowing $1000, the risk is a lot lower because you have 100 borrowers. You don't have what's called idiosyncratic risk, which you do have on corporate loans. That's why I really like asset-backed loans: there's often more of a diversified pool of collateral and, when it's structured the right way, lots of security and subordination underneath.

As you can see from figure 6.1, the way a portfolio asset-backed loan works is, you've got a company and all they do is borrow a large amount of money, then lend lots of small amounts of money to lots of borrowers. They earn interest and take security, with the revenue being the NIM (net interest margin), which is the difference in the interest rate they earn on lots of small loans minus the interest they pay away on the big loan. I've used cars in the example, but it could be anything. It could be roofs or pools, but the company needs to get money somehow in order to lend the $1000 to lots of people buying cars. What we do at iPartners is lend money to that special purpose company and say, 'We'll lend you the money as long as all you do with it is lend it to people looking to buy cars, and you don't lend an amount greater than $1000 per person. We'll also only lend you the money if you put in 10 per cent (in my example $10 000) as equity (loss protection), and you are subordinate to us, so you lose money before we do. We need you to be aligned with iPartners in structure.' This can also be referred to as the loss protection or subordination that sits underneath our exposure.

Continuing with this example, if five of those loans fall over and the first $10 000 was put in by the company we've loaned to, it doesn't affect us because the loss ($5000) is going to the company that originated them. Nobody enjoys losses, but that company expects that of 100 loans a few of them probably won't get repaid. The profitability they make from lending to 100 people is typically great enough to offset the fact that they're going to lose some money over time. As the lender (investor) in this loan, we've got quite a secure position because we've got 100 borrowers on a full recourse basis that can be collected on.

There are 100 cars sitting there in security, and there's $10 000, or 10 per cent of equity capital, underneath, protecting our position. So we've got a senior secured position on a finance company. That finance company does nothing other than lend money, pay interest to the people financing it and earn interest from the people who have borrowed from it. It's a very simple business, which is why it's my preferred risk in the credit asset class.

Asset-backed lending could also be a single asset such as a big truck (there's more risk in a single asset) — see, for example, figure 6.2 (overleaf). iPartners would lend money to a person who wants to buy a big truck and we would take a registered charge on their truck. That way, if they don't pay our interest and money back, we would become the proud owner of a big truck and could keep it and/or sell it to recoup the proceeds of the loan. This is heaps better than being unsecured. This again creates a fixed-income investment because we are earning interest.

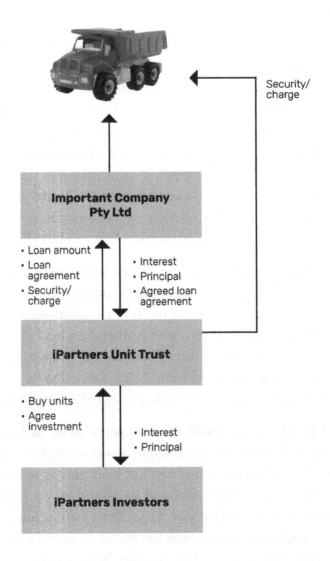

Figure 6.2 Asset-backed lending to a single asset

Asset-backed senior, junior and mezzanine debt

Let's now complicate this example of the car finance company to explain the different types of asset-backed loans where you lend over a portfolio of loans and offer three tranches of loans, effectively providing a capital stack. You can give senior secured, mezzanine secured and junior secured loans all over the same pool of security, as shown in figure 6.3 (overleaf).

Let's say the company has $10 000 of equity and $90 000 of debt, meaning there's $100 000 of capital that can be deployed for the company to run. That $90 000 of debt can be tranched for different types of investors.

Let's say there's a junior secured loan of $10 000. This loan would sit above the $10 000 of equity, with the next $10 000 coming from the junior secured lender. What this means is that if there are losses greater than $10 000, the junior secured lender (investor) is potentially exposed. They're effectively lending the amount of money from $10 000 to $20 000. Talking percentages, that means 10 per cent to 20 per cent tranche of the finance funding company is junior secured.

Next is a mezzanine tranche, which is a loan in the middle, from $20 000 to $40 000, or 20 per cent to 40 per cent. So that investor has exposure of any losses from $20 000 to $40 000.

Next is the senior position, which would take everything else ($40 000 to $100 000) senior secured. When you take the senior secured position in that transaction, there is $40 000 of capital sitting below you before your first dollar of loss. That's the senior security, taking that 40 per cent to 100 per cent.

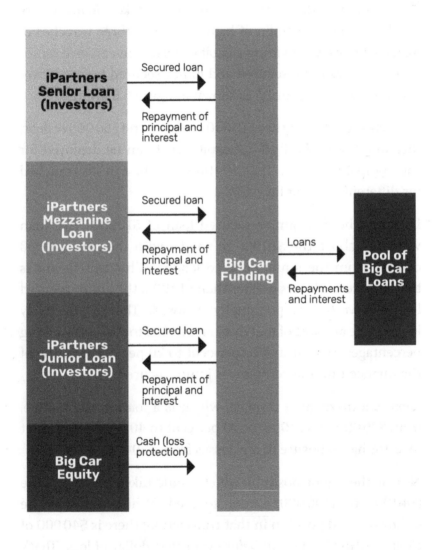

Figure 6.3 Tranched lending

The logic behind these different types of loans is simply that they create different investable assets, depending on the risk profile of the investors. In private markets you have investors that want higher returns and higher risk. The high-return, high-risk people will go into the junior secured tranche of these deals. They're saying, 'I reckon 10 per cent equity subordination from this finance company is enough. I'm happy to take the next 10 per cent of risk if you pay me 12 per cent interest for the pleasure.'

Then you've got senior lenders, who say, 'I'm pretty conservative. I want someone else to take the first $40 000 of losses before me. I'm happy to get paid 7 per cent interest. I've got a junior and mezzanine loan below me taking the risk above equity. I sit right at the top of the capital structure as the senior secured lender, and this suits me. I'm happy to earn less interest for the lower risk.'

Offering investors the choice to invest across different parts of the capital stack can create a more efficient and lower average interest rate for the borrower because tranching lowers the risk of the senior secured tranche to the point that investors are happy to receive a lower return.

Example of tranched asset-backed lending

In chapter 2, I described the trade iPartners did with a company that lends money to parents to pay for their kids' private education. This is a great example of tranched asset-backed lending. We did a two-year junior and senior loan, with the junior loan paying 12 per cent and the senior loan paying 6 per cent. The security was their portfolio of loans. That was the asset that backed the loan. And we rank senior in the capital structure to them, so we've got a lot of protection.

Receivables finance asset-backed loans

Think of an accountant who deals with small businesses, doing all their accounting monthly, and their clients take 90 days to pay. They have 'accounts receivables' on their own company books, meaning there are lots of small businesses that owe them money, which will get paid sometime in the next 90 days. Let's say their accounts receivables totals $5 million, from 2000 different businesses. I might tell that accountant, 'Look, I'll give you 95 per cent of your receivables today upfront, which is $4.75 million, in exchange for all the money you're owed that's going to come in over the next 90 days. And I'm going to take security over all of your receivables. Then, as your clients pay you, that money goes to me to repay the money I gave you upfront.'

So the accountant is owed $5 million, which will get paid at some point in the next 90 days. I give them a $4.75 million loan today, then all the payments over the next 90 days come to me and I expect that they add up to at least $4.75 million plus the interest I am owed. That's an example of an asset-backed receivables loan. It uses the receivables as the asset backing, and the asset behind it is the receivables from 2000 different companies. The accountant wants the money today to manage their cash flow, which is why they do it. These sorts of transactions have been done for years by finance companies, family offices, institutions and banks.

As I've mentioned before, the primary difference between public markets and alternatives (private markets) is that public investing markets over the years have been so much easier to access. Our business is about making alternative assets — that is, all the other stuff — as easy to access as equities. The reason investors haven't been doing it is because they don't know how to find it, and if they do, they don't know how to package it. Also, they often don't have the time to do the work involved. So we take the time to find and package these opportunities, and to simplify them for our investors. We'll go to them and say, 'Do you want to invest in a one-year unit trust that's paying you 10 per cent per annum? It's backed by the security of the receivables of this accounting firm.' Our job is taking something complex and to a degree simplifying it so investors can get access.

Agriculture asset-backed lending

Asset-backed debt can also work for agricultural businesses. It's the same as the car finance company example. You just replace cars with cows. iPartners has a trade where we've financed a $100 million facility for farmers to buy cattle. They buy calves, feed them and then take them to the market. From an asset class perspective, it's quite a good asset class for investors. If you have a portfolio of cars as your security, when the car goes down in value, so does your security. If you have a portfolio full of fattening cattle, the actual value goes up every week (assuming stable market pricing) because they gain weight. Cattle, especially fattening cattle, are an awesome asset class to lend against for this reason. (Of course, if the borrower doesn't pay interest or repay the loan, we'll be turning up with our truck, picking up the cattle and taking them to market to recoup our money.)

Another agriculture example is crops. You fund the cost of seed for a particular season, and then you have security of the output of that seed being planted. You lend the money upfront, the asset goes up over time and you ultimately get paid back at the end of the cycle (in theory, of course).

Whether cows or cars, the investment approach is the same

Whether an investor comes along and wants to buy an investment backed by cars, or by cows or crops, the investment is exactly the same. It's an investment that pays them interest over a period of time, has a maturity, has security and if all goes well, they get their money back and go on to another investment.

The underlying collateral can change, but the piece that makes it investable for investors doesn't change. It's just a nice little unit trust that pays interest — and investors get reports, valuations and everything you expect from a listed equity.

Asset-backed lending in the debt space is by far my preferred area to invest in. It's a bit more complex to document and it's a bit harder to find and recognise the assets. It's also a bit more complex to come up with an investable product, but this is what makes it attractive. Those barriers mean there's a scarcity of capital investing in that space. Wherever there's a scarcity of capital, I can typically get a return over and above what you would expect for the given risk — it's basic supply and demand.

There's money to be made for investors in complexity. If you can understand the complexity and simplify it so the product becomes investable, you can generate really attractive returns for the risks because other parties either don't have the experience or the knowledge to simplify it in a way that makes sense to investors.

Structured products and structured notes

The terms 'structured products' and 'structured notes' are used interchangeably. These products typically involve combining a debt obligation (often simply a term deposit or bond) with a derivative such as a call option (which is a type of derivative that gives the investor the right, but not the obligation, to participate in the positive performance of an underlying asset). Investors buy structured products because they can obtain a more tailored investment than that obtained from traditional investments.

There are a few different types of structured products, including credit- and equity-linked notes, which we'll look into in this chapter. There's also the option of having structured products with tax efficiency. It can get a bit complicated so I'm not going to dig too deep into all the types of structured product. The following examples will give you an overview.

Equity-linked notes

Equity-linked notes are a type of structured product where the return you get is linked to the performance of the underlying equity or equity index. They are usually structured so that you get your initial investment back, plus a variable return that depends on the performance of the linked equity. They are also known as 'zero + call' structures. This is because they combine a deposit (the fixed-income portion) with a call option. The deposit earns zero interest until maturity, when the call option kicks in.

Let's say someone has $100 to invest and they want an investment that has principal protection and provides equity upside. The issuer of the structured note could put $90 of that into something like a zero coupon term deposit with ANZ with a three-year maturity, which will return $100 in three years. That's the fixed-income portion. Then the issuer of the structured note will take the $10 difference and buy a call option on, say, the ASX 200 to give investors the potential for upside. (The ASX 200 is an index of the top 200 companies listed on the Australian Stock Exchange.) That investor now has an investment where they know for sure that in three years they will get their money back *and* the $10 difference has bought them, say, 1.5 call options on the ASX 200.

The 1.5 call option means they have 150 per cent participation in the upside of the ASX 200 from today. This means that if equity markets go up 1 per cent, they get a return of 1.5 per cent. So if equity markets are up 100 per cent in three years, they're up 150 per cent. They get a 150 per cent return on their money and the bank gives them their $100 back from the deposit (unless the bank was in default — then it's not that simple). But if the equity market is down three years later, they will get 100 per cent of their money back from the bank, so there's no loss. In this synthetic way (hence why it's called a 'structured note') they're able to have limited risk on their principal (an opportunity cost), with a potential upside from the call option.

To broaden this example, the issuer on behalf of the investor could spend the call option premium (that $10) on all sorts of things. They could, for example, buy a call option on oil, gold or a single-company listed equity.

Having explained all of this, it's worth noting that if you go to a bank — at the time of writing — for a three-year deposit, you'll only get a 2.5 per cent per annum return (rates are currently going up). You'll have to put down $92.50 (not $90) for it to mature to $100 (strictly 2.5 per cent per annum with annual compounding, you need $92.86, [the maths $(1 / (1 + 2.5\%)^3) \times \$100$] but we are ignoring compounding for the purpose of examples). This means you'll only have 7.5 per cent to spend on a call option. Instead, let's use the iPartners Core Income Fund as an example, which is returning around 6 per cent per annum across three years, generating approximately 18 per cent. This means today you could put $82 (again ignoring compounding) into that fund, and at three years' maturity expect to get around $100 back. This gives you $18 to spend on call options, which means instead of buying 1.5 call options, you could potentially buy 2.5 call options on the ASX 200.

So you can see that the benefit of that higher return from the credit fund (over the bank zero coupon note) can be used to potentially purchase more optionality.

(The trade-off is you are now also taking on a higher risk profile on your return of principal.)

At the moment, at iPartners we're looking at offering this, but we'll have a 12-month investment instead of three years until maturity. So investors will put about $94 into our credit fund, which is specifically called the Core Income Fund. That will be used at 6 per cent to purchase a call option on the ASX 200. The investor knows, worst case, they should get $100 back at the end of the year. Best case, they get their $100 back, plus the upside on the ASX 200. It's pretty sweet when it works! That's structured products — they can be highly tailored to suit investor appetite.

How does this compare to simply investing $100 in the ASX 200?

When you put $100 on the stock market, if the market is down by 20 per cent, you're down by 20 per cent; if it's up by 20 per cent, you're up by 20 per cent. But with a structured note trade, you are less concerned if the market is down by 20 per cent because you have limited downside on your call option. With a call option, the worst thing you could lose is the premium you pay. You don't have any downside exposure. (If you sell a call option, it's a different story.) This is how, with alternative assets, you can create a risk profile that suits the investor.

Why do banks do zero coupons?

Banks do these trades because they are deposits. Banks love deposits because they get cheap funding from investor mums and dads, and then lend it to other mums and dads — at a higher interest rate — for their mortgages. The banks sit in the middle, taking a clip on the way through. A bank will (at the moment) only pay 2 to 4 per cent interest on a deposit, but they'll lend that money to someone else for their home loan at 4 to 6 per cent, so the bank makes a 2 per cent net interest margin (they do obviously have other costs too though, so it's not quite that straightforward).

Equity-linked notes with a twist

One of the more popular and riskier equity-linked notes in the private wealth arena sees investors selling options (loss can be large) in a structured note rather than buying options (loss limited to the option premium).

In the simplest sense and best-case scenario an investor will invest $100 for 12 months and be paid a high fixed coupon of typically more than 10 per cent (creating a fixed interest type payoff profile — higher equity volatility tends to mean a higher coupon). Then, on the risk side, they will take downside exposure to the performance of, say, two listed equities by selling a put on the worst performing share (you will remember from the section on options that when you sell a put you are providing someone else with insurance; the further the share falls the worse it gets for you!).

If one of the equities was to fall too far in price terms (equity-linked notes tend to have no downside exposure until one of the shares falls by more than 30 per cent, for example) you become exposed to the downside performance of the share (as you sold the outright put).

In summary, when it works, you get a nice return and your money back; when it doesn't work, you could lose your entire principal.

For example, say you had an equity-linked note with exposure to ANZ and BHP (two listed Australian companies) through selling the put, and one of these shares was to fall 55 per cent from its current price. On maturity, you would expect to only get back 45 per cent of your investment plus your coupon (a bad outcome). If one fell 63 per cent, you would get back 37 per cent plus your coupon (an even worse outcome, although you would typically outperform compared to owning the shares outright as your coupon would typically be greater than the dividend yield, so not all bad!). Otherwise, in the best-case scenario, if both shares were to perform better than a 30 per cent fall you could expect to get 100 per cent of your investment plus your coupon (the best-case outcome), meaning you have no upside benefit to the equities.

I have tried to keep this as a high-level overview. There are all sorts of permutations to these notes: different maturities, barriers (e.g. the 30 per cent scenario above), shares, number of companies, currencies and asset classes).

There is a place for these investments with more experienced investors because they enable them to tailor their investments to their specific investment views and generate a more fixed-income-like investment from equity markets with returns above that achieved through simply receiving dividends. However, the payoffs can be contrived at times: the pricing can be skewed in the issuer's favour and it can be hard to check the relative value and complex to unwind early.

I would recommend, if you're considering these types of investments, that you are sure to partner with someone who understands option pricing and dealing with investment banks and brokers to navigate you through the potential pitfalls.

Credit-linked notes

Prior to the GFC, credit-linked notes were prevalent. They have made a bit of a comeback, but not to pre-GFC volumes.

A credit-linked note is basically a synthetic corporate bond that combines selling a credit default swap with the debt obligation. (Under a credit default swap you provide someone with insurance against a default in a large, typically listed, company's senior unsecured bonds. You are taking the risk of a default and as such get compensated for the risk with a premium stream and the risk closely reflects owning the bond.) The investor's return, which is fixed income in nature, is a combination of the return on the credit default swap and the debt obligation. The debt obligation could again simply be a bank term deposit.

A seller of a credit default swap is going long risk and effectively providing a third-party insurance (to the buyer of the credit default swap) on a default event by a company on its debt.

For example, say BHP has a five-year bond trading in the market, and the owner of the bond was nervous that BHP may default. They could buy credit default swap protection (and pay a premium) to the seller of credit default protection (say, from the credit-linked note investor). If the default was to occur, the buyer could claim on the credit-linked note investor to compensate them for the loss on the physical BHP bond holding. If the bond does not default, the buyer of the protection would have paid a premium for no benefit, which makes it behave a bit like an insurance contract and potentially generates an attractive return for the credit-linked note investor.

For an investor, the credit-linked note tends to replicate the economic risk of owning the underlying bond, although it can be tailored to better suit the investor preferences through, for example, removing the currency risk (if the underlying bond is denominated in a foreign currency) and offering a shorter maturity.

Structured products with tax efficiency

There are a number of types of structured product with tax efficiency. We'll take a look at one example, a protected equity loan, to explain the overall idea of how they can work. This is a tax-efficient product that has lots of quirks, turns and twists.

There are two tax rules in Australia that make this investment mildly tax efficient. First, as with most investments where you borrow to invest, the interest is potentially tax deductible if the investment is made primarily for the purpose of generating taxable income. Second, if the asset is owned for longer than 12 months, you can potentially access discounted capital gains tax. So let's say in the month of May you buy a basket of Australian equities. You then also buy a put option on those equities (as discussed in chapter 5, a put option is a kind of insurance that protects you from loss if the equity goes down — in this case you are the buyer). Say the put option costs about 7 per cent of the price of the equities. Now, because the put option removes the downside risk, you may be able to borrow 100 per cent of the cost of that equity from a friendly bank or other credit provider, such as iPartners. Because you own the equity, you are entitled to the upside on it, and potentially the dividends and franking credits (this is no different from buying most Aussie equities), and because you purchased the put option, you have limited downside.

In Australia, interest paid upfront is potentially tax deductible for the upcoming 12 months. Because you bought it in May, coming up to the end of the tax year, if you prepay the interest, you could get a tax deduction for that year for the interest that was paid to generate taxable income. And if you own that equity for longer than 12 months, and the equity goes up, then you're potentially entitled to the discount CGT if you sell the asset, but you may also continue to own the asset. That is quite a common structure in Australia.

There is some risk involved, but only on what you paid upfront. The put option in this example costs you 7 per cent, the interest costs you, say, 6 per cent and there's a profit margin built in for the lender. Your risk is that you pay 13 per cent upfront (7 per cent put option + 6 per cent interest) and the equity goes down. After receiving your dividends and franking, say that's 5 per cent, you've just lost 8 per cent because the equity hasn't gone up (maybe less after taking into account any interest and tax deduction). The equity has to go up for you to actually make money, but your risk is somewhat reduced due to owning the put option. Your maximum absolute loss is equal to the 13 per cent you pay upfront, minus the dividends and franking (if entitled) that you earn, minus the tax deduction you got upfront for the interest (if any). The maximum upside is unlimited.

Note: there are specific rules around deductibility of interest on principal protected product, which in short means that not all of it is deductible. Check with your accountant, or if you want to be more DIY, it's written nicely in tax legislation if you do a quick search.

The pay-off is great once the equity performance is above the break-even (that is, the return required to recoup the after-tax cost of the investment) as you have borrowed 100 per cent, so you have significant leverage.

Assuming that the total cost to enter the investment after tax was 8 per cent, the equity would need to be up 8 per cent to break even. If the market was up 24 per cent, that would be a 200 per cent return on your net investment. Leverage is great when asset performance goes in your favour.

If you're confident that the equity is going to go up, it's a low-risk way to have a really leveraged play on a stock. Your risk is that if the stock doesn't go up, you definitely lose money, but it can be a tax-efficient way to do it because of the way it's been put together. The key thing about these types of trades is that they are a genuine investment first. Investors need to go in thinking they're an investment (because unless the equities go up you will lose money).

A last word on structured notes

As you can see, structured notes are quite complex. And I've only touched on a few here. You could combine an FX (foreign exchange rate), interest rate, commodity, cryptocurrency and various combinations of these to create a tailored structured note pay-off to suit investor appetite. As long as there is a derivative market it's likely you could do a structured note. A key piece of advice on derivatives is that even though you can unwind them early, it's typically unadvisable to do so because unwinding the pieces can be expensive, involve crossing spreads (in simple terms this means effectively paying a fee when you buy the derivative and another fee to sell it back) and is often a profit-making exercise for the issuer of the structured notes.

Chapter 8

Infrastructure

Infrastructure is a pretty hard asset class to access for normal investors because the asset size and valuations are typically very large, so it lends itself to big institutional investors and fund managers controlling the market and access. There are two primary types of infrastructure assets you can invest in and they both big: economic infrastructure and social infrastructure.

Economic infrastructure includes things such as toll roads, bridges, railways and airports. They are physical assets that are typically government owned but can be owned by the private sector. They tend to exist in an environment where the user is paying, whether they know it or not, and have very long payback periods for the owners with at times monopoly-like rights for the use. An example would be a toll road owned by Transurban (an Australian listed company that manages and develops toll roads) where they charge each car a toll for use.

Social infrastructure is mainly government-owned buildings such as schools, hospitals, prisons and government offices that the end user typically doesn't or can't pay for directly. They are funded through taxes and possibly public private partnerships (PPP) where the project has a heavily debt-funded element backed by government cash flows and operates through a partnership between the government and the private sector.

Infrastructure equity and debt

With infrastructure, like other asset classes, you can invest in the equity, debt or a hybrid instrument of infrastructure projects. When you invest in equity, you're paying to own a piece of the infrastructure, so you will own, for example, part of the big bridge. When you invest in debt — usually senior or junior secured debt — you're giving a loan so someone else can own the big bridge.

Let's say there's a new fancy bridge going to be built. The equity investors come in and put in their equity, so they own the bridge. Then the debt investors come along and say, 'I'll do a senior secured loan (these loans are discussed in chapter 6) at 70 per cent LVR. I'm going to take this bridge as security, so until you pay me back, I've got security over this bridge.' It's a straightforward senior secured loan, but instead of having, say, a house as security, you've got a bridge.

How do I invest in infrastructure?

As mentioned, infrastructure is a hard one for a single-person investor to get access to. They are usually enormous assets worth huge amounts of money. The only real way to access diversified infrastructure investments is through a fund that has billions of dollars to invest. The large super funds in Australia have traditionally been the ones involved in infrastructure. Platforms such as iPartners, though, are starting to bridge this access gap.

Back in the 1990s there were infrastructure funds such as Macquarie Infrastructure launching in Australia, which were interesting. The average investor can also access infrastructure by buying listed equities that own or develop the infrastructure, such as Transurban, or by investing in global unlisted funds or the few local private infrastructure funds. If you visit your friendly financial planner about infrastructure, they'll say, 'Buy this local infrastructure fund', which tends to be a fund of lots of listed equities, although they may give you some exposure to unlisted assets.

The key piece to infrastructure is that if you take equity in it via a listed operating business, you take on operational risk rather than pure exposure to the physical asset. You could take units in a listed infrastructure fund, and you can also invest in single infrastructure funds via a platform such as iPartners.

A cool one that was done on the iPartners platform gave investors exposure to an airport in the UK.

Example of a UK airport trade

A large infrastructure fund that is an enormous fund manager worth billions of dollars had a UK airport in its portfolio and wanted to sell a majority stake. It set up a new fund (a sidecar fund) to purchase the airport, and via the iPartners platform and a local fund manager, investors were able to get exposure to a very small portion of it.

It was done through a global co-investment vehicle or co-investment fund ('vehicle' and 'fund' tend to be interchangeable, even though they can be different legal structures) and

(continued)

Australian investors got access because a local manager was offering investors access through the iPartners platform. So the global manager put the asset into a separate fund, and got lots of other investors to buy it. Australian local investors also got access to a small allocation of the multibillion-dollar asset sale. Like I said, the numbers in infrastructure are huge! We were such a small player so it was amazing that local direct investors got access to a slice of this pie. I think it's cool that there are Aussie investors who, via our platform, own a tiny bit of a UK airport. It's something they wouldn't traditionally get to invest in because it's a very hard asset to get exposure to.

This was an equity investment. Figure 8.1 is a simple diagram explaining how iPartners fit into the big picture.

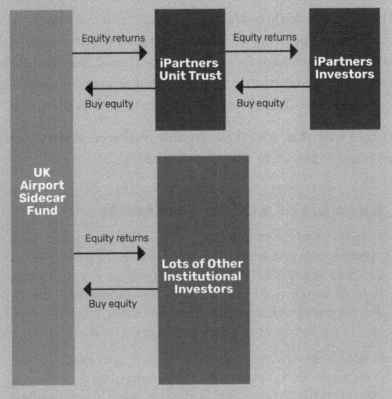

Figure 8.1 UK airport investment structure

Public private partnerships (PPPs)

A PPP is a partnership between the public and private sectors where the government partners with the private sector to deliver infrastructure and related services over the long term, with a risk-sharing arrangement. The private sector builds the infrastructure and operates (or contracts to operate) the asset over the duration. This creates investment opportunities for investors who plan to live a long time!

The debt in PPPs (often 20 to 30 years) is quite investable. It tends to be a long-dated and lower return asset, and typically has some form of CPI (inflation) linkage. This could be a Capital Indexed Bond (CIB), where the capital to be repaid accretes with inflation — a little bit zero coupon bond like, but accreting at the variable rate of inflation — or it could be an Index Annuity Bond (IAB), where your coupon ratchets up at the rate of inflation, so over time you would expect your absolute coupon to go up.

The equity for these projects usually remains with the project sponsor, or group of sponsors, who tend to be very large institutional investors or infrastructure funds, which is why access is limited to buying the equity in listed infrastructure companies or infrastructure funds.

Chapter 9

Commodities

Commodities are a great alternative asset class because they tend to have a low correlation to other assets. With some commodities — for example, gold or silver — you can buy the actual thing and put it in your cupboard or safe. With other commodities — such as corn, oil and wheat — you've got the cost of storage and wastage, and there's the risk that it can go off (spoilage). So financial instruments have been created to give you exposure to commodities without having to physically own and store them yourself. In this section I'll run you through everything there is to know about investing in commodities.

Why are commodities a good investment?

The real attraction with commodities is that they often have hedge-like characteristics (risk reducing on a portfolio basis). This means they have a low correlation to other asset classes — that is, they tend to perform well when other assets can be underperforming. Taking exposure to something like energy or agriculture commodities can be a nice way to offset inflation. If you're long (meaning you have a positive pay-off from a positive price move) and you have exposure to agricultural futures or commodities, then as inflation goes up, these commodities tend to go up too. It's a nice hedge against other asset classes — such as fixed rate bonds — that might go down in price in an inflationary environment.

Commodities is an asset class where you can take exposure by buying the physical equity of companies involved in the sector. To do this, you need to find a listed company that grows and produces corn or wheat, or whatever you're looking for, and buy its equity. The problem with buying the listed equity is that you don't really get the pure price return of the underlying commodity because it gets clouded with the operational risk in the business. If the business growing the corn is run badly, even if corn as a commodity goes through the roof you may not actually get that gain because of bad management. This is why a lot of investors prefer to have real direct exposure to corn and other commodities.

The number-one way that people get exposure to commodities is via futures contracts.

Futures

Futures contracts are the easiest and most common way to get exposure to lots of different commodities. You don't have to buy a whole pile of corn (for example) and store it in your shed. You can buy a futures contract on corn. It gives you synthetic exposure. There are futures contracts on equity indexes, bond prices — and lots of other things — and they're heavily used in commodities. Ultimately, over time, futures track the price of the commodities and you don't have to physically buy them (as long as the contract is closed out before maturity).

What are commodity futures?

A commodity future is the future price of a commodity.

Think of a future like an index where you're taking exposure at the prevailing price. That price, from a futures perspective, is the price at which you can buy the real thing at a date in the future. It's a bit tricky to get your head around, so it helps to look at a real-world situation first.

You've got a corn farmer who's a bit worried that the price of corn is about to fall through the floor. So they sell the corn three months forward at the prevailing forward price. If corn does fall, the farmer has made money on the futures contract, which should partially offset making less money from their real corn sale because this farmer has to turn up at the real market and actually sell the corn. If the market goes down, they get less money for their corn, but because they've actually sold corn already, they've made some money on their futures contract (they would close this contract out before maturity and cash settle any gains or losses).

So most of these things initially existed for real producers and consumers to hedge their risk. Simply put, the consumer is buying the corn, and the producer is growing the corn.

The company that makes corn soup has to buy the corn from the farmer. It has a view that corn will increase to $750 in a month's time, so it locks in the current futures price of $650 with a futures contract. The soup manufacturer could be right or wrong, but they have a real need. They are going to have to turn up and buy that corn from the farmer at a real price. If it's gone through the roof, they lose on the physical trade but win on the futures trade.

There's a clearing house in between that reduces the counterparty credit risk (the risk that the futures buyer or seller cannot settle its obligations). How can the soup manufacturer be sure the corn producer will honour their contract? The clearing house ensures that each party does what is required to settle the contract and it requires initial margin to offset any potential move in the futures price, along with a variation margin to be posted over time if the price moves too far away from the expected variation.

That's a real-world need, but there are also investors who sometimes get involved in futures like this simply because they're bored and feel like they want to punt on something else. They predict, 'I think corn is going to go through the roof.' So they start buying the futures contract. If they're right, they make money and if they're wrong, they lose money. So the speculators and traders join in. Speculators and traders can swing the entire market around at times, depending on the liquidity of the underlying commodity or index. They are a significant part of the market.

The problem with outright futures is that you have to do things like post margin (you would post additional margin if you were losing money on your futures contract, to retain your position) and frequently update margin. It can be hard if you're looking for a set-and-forget type of investment to get exposure to commodities.

You can access various futures contracts through brokers and banks.

The nuts and bolts of how futures contracts work

With futures, you have to put a margin down. If you try to trade a futures contract today and want to buy it at $10, and then it goes to $8, well you've lost $2 on that contract because you agreed to buy it at $10. You've got a mark-to-market loss. (Mark-to-market means the difference between the current fair value of the futures contract and your initial trade price.) Because of this, the clearing house (when you first enter the futures contract) will make you lodge collateral upfront to cover the possible mark-to-market loss. If the market starts going against you, you'll have to keep lodging more collateral to ensure the clearing house doesn't have credit risk against you when it comes time to settle the futures contract. If you fail to lodge the collateral, your futures contract gets closed out.

To settle a futures contract you just have to offset it. You bought the future, so you sell the same contract and they cancel out.

The margin concept is critical for the futures market; otherwise there would be defaults everywhere. If someone bought futures and the market went against them, they could just hang up the phone and run. But because the clearing house has their collateral, people don't run — and if they did, it wouldn't matter because the clearing house has the collateral, so they would simply sell their position and take their collateral to offset the transaction on the other side.

The investor who doesn't feel like trading futures to access commodities can get a more passive access via a structured note, which we looked at in chapter 6. They do this by combining a debt obligation with a derivative or a futures contract as a more set-and-forget approach, which may even be using a commodity index.

Commodity indexes

Futures is a key part of investing in commodities. You can invest in single commodities, or you can invest in commodity indexes, which can be more popular with passive investors.

A commodity index is simply a basket of different commodity futures contracts often administered by a bank or a broker to make it easier for investors. These futures contracts are often for oil, corn, wheat, gold or silver, as they are the prime commodities.

The thing about commodity indexes is this: you never take delivery of the commodities. The index owner rolls over (rolls) your futures contract for you as it's coming up to expiring. So, say I have a one-month contract. Rather than settling it after one month, I'll roll it into the next futures contract (sell the shorter maturing contract and buy the longer maturity contract). So, the manager of the index rolls the commodity, typically to the next futures contract, using a predefined rule.

They do this because investors may want to be invested in perpetuity. The idea of commodity indexes is that you want to take exposure to the market over time. If commodities in general gallop, you win. If they go down, you lose. The only way you can stay invested is to continually roll that futures contract.

But there are all sorts of complexities in rolling futures contracts. There are two different types of curves when you roll with commodities: contango and backwardation.

Contango is an upward sloping curve. For example, if the price of corn in month 1 is $100, in month 2 it's $110 and in month 3 it's $130. That's the shape of the contango curve. Backwardation is a downward curve. For example, corn is at $90 in month 1, $80 in month 2 and $70 in month 3.

As the days pass, depending on how the curve shapes, you can either make money or lose money from the roll. Backwardation is the best curve to make money on. Say the spot price is around $100 today, you bought the three-month futures at $70 and nothing happened across the three months to the curve shape. You would get to close out the contract at $100 on the maturity date and you made $30 from not really doing anything.

The key point is that, depending on the shape of the futures curve, investors can lose or make money from rolling to the next contract. The roll is a key element of returns in investing in commodities.

First-, second- and third- generation indexes

For those who get excited by detail, commodity indexes have been changing over time. The first-generation index was pretty much, 'Let's just roll each month. Let's keep this exposure going for investors. If it goes up, investors do okay.' Then you get these smart bankers and funds with mathematical models that try to work out how to make money from that roll. Instead of being mechanical and just rolling on the seventh day (for example) regardless of what the markets are doing, they might say, 'Let's roll at any point across 14 days, and just trade the day that minimises the loss from the roll, or maximises the gain from the roll.'

Second-generation indexes attempt to maximise the money you can make from your roll strategy.

Third generation is maximising the benefits of the roll as well as maximising the percentage allocation to the constituents of the index. Pretty much bored quants (mathematical geniuses!) got us to this point. The quants used their financial models to work out how to best construct an index, what the index weightings are and other index construction criteria. They then use this financial model to determine how to maximise the roll as well as maximise the weighting or percentage allocation of the various constituents of the index. That's commodity indexes.

Either way, commodity indices or funds are quite a nice way for investors to take a passive exposure to the commodity asset class and benefit from its diversification benefits.

Agriculture

We touched on agriculture in chapter 4 (the chapter on property) as large elements of agriculture investment are simply investment in the real asset of land, whether it be a debt or equity exposure. Agriculture is also one of the most common commodities in Australia, and a fast-growing asset class for investors, so it is worth digging into deeper here (excuse the pun). We at iPartners have limited direct investment in raw agricultural commodities but there are numerous other ways to invest, including agricultural futures contracts (covered in the last section), senior secured loans and other forms of loans over rural assets, asset-backed finance, equity in operating businesses, asset aggregation strategies and purchase of land with a lease back to the operator. Let's take a look at a few of these.

Senior secured loan over rural assets

Say a farmer wants to buy their neighbour's farm but they can't get a bank loan. At iPartners we would say, 'I'll do a senior loan for you to purchase the neighbour's farm as long as you put in enough equity to do the purchase.' It's like a home loan, but they're not buying a house, they're buying an operating farm and assets to expand production. Where the bank decided it was too out of the box and didn't want to lend to them, we look at the fact that they're an existing established farming family who are very successful and want to buy their neighbour's farm. It ticks a lot of boxes: they're putting in equity, they're growing their business and they have a good track record. So we're happy to do a senior loan for them.

We will likely do the loan for a short period of time — say, eight months. The idea is that they'll use our money to merge the farms, then they'll go back to the bank and say, 'Well, it's a lot less risky now because we have merged the two businesses and demonstrated profitability. Will you refinance us?' The bank will then come in with cheaper funding, probably at 5 to 6 per cent, but the farmers were happy to pay the higher interest to us for a short period of time to get the purchase of the neighbour's farm done. So the investment from our perspective is indirectly in commodities, specifically debt over agricultural land. The investment itself is a bridge-type facility.

We are, at the time of writing, looking at doing an investment just like this for a cattle asset in New South Wales.

Example of cattle financing

There's a cattle financier we work with that is a non-bank lender providing capital to farmers to buy fattening cattle. We lend money to them so they have the capital to lend money out to farmers. For example, the farmer buys 50 young steers and sells them as mature cattle after they've put on roughly 2 to 3 kilograms a week for maybe six months. The value of the asset, the cattle, goes up. Then they sell the cattle. The farmer is buying and selling, and we're financing the purchase of the steers. Once the cattle go to market, the loan gets repaid and they repeat the process.

The best way to think about it is literally as cattle financing. We've provided about $100 million to these guys. It returns about 10 per cent per annum for our investors, and it's an 18-month maturity.

This funding model can be used for many other forms of agricultural produce, such as crops and sheep. It's a form of asset-backed lending.

Agriculture operating businesses

Another way iPartners look to invest in agriculture is directly in a single operating business and/or the aggregation of agricultural operating businesses to become a larger portfolio size. Or, to put it more simply: buying lots of farms and aggregating them into a single investment structure. The more farms you have, the more scalable you can make the farming business and potentially the more attractive it is to a buyer down the track.

The expected return from an operating farm can be broken down into three parts: the appreciation of the land that the farm is on; the operating business and how efficient it is; and the returns from the produce (crops or stocks). When the asset (the land and/or the operating business) goes up in value, there's a non-cash flow return through the accretion (increase) in the asset's value instead of purely a cash return per annum, which you would typically expect on a traditional fixed-income instrument. When there's both a yield and value accretion, it's measured using what's called internal rate of return (IRR). In simple terms, you can think of it as a total return per year.

Example of Tasmanian dairy farms

We did a fund with a Tasmanian dairy farm aggregator. They came to us to raise $20 million for the fund. We did about $5 million of it by aggregating our investors, who now effectively own a portion of some Tasmanian dairy farms — real land, assets and the operations. The aggregation part is that they've simply bought a number of dairy farms and continued to aggregate them. They are now up to four farms. It's essentially the same investment strategy as the rural pubs trade discussed in chapter 4. The investor is an armchair owner of a portion of a dairy farm and a portion of a portfolio of its funds. The target return on that is about 15 per cent IRR per annum until the exit (the simplest way to think of that is around 15 per cent per year).

One of the biggest risks in an operating business is the quality and experience of the operator. Before we make a longer term investment in an operating business, a significant portion of our due diligence is on assessing the ability of the operator. The operator is usually the driver behind the yield over time and operational improvements. The passive land accretion (increase in value) is partly market driven and less under the operator's or investor's control.

Real land and operating leases

This strategy is relatively simple. You buy a real asset — a farm, for example — then you lease it to an operator or farmer who pays you a regular lease payment. It is an agricultural version of owning an investment property. Over time you hope the asset goes up and your tenant — the producer or farmer — continues to pay you rent.

A last word on commodities

When inflation rises, commodities, particularly agriculture and energy, are an awesome hedge to inflation. Inflation is something a lot of investors care about. It can potentially kill the value of money, killing the value of your savings. If you know there is inflation, you know commodity and asset prices will potentially go up. And you want your returns and your performance to go up with inflation at the very least. Commodities in general have also been found to have a lower correlation to other asset classes, so they can help diversify an investment portfolio and potentially help reduce the portfolio risk.

International access funds

Pretty much everything I have described to this point can be accessed via an alternative fund run by iPartners, a fund manager, or managers, locally in Australia or internationally. They would simply offer you a diversified assortment rather than single-asset exposure. It can be an interesting way to invest for more passive set-and-forget investors.

Offshore funds

There is a definite drive for investors to access offshore brand-name (large, global, experienced) alternative investment managers. This growth is being primarily driven by iPartners-like technology, with providers aggregating this investor demand to the required market parcel. These large managers often have minimum investment amounts (market parcels) of between $10 million and $25 million per investor. This is a quantum that very few investors can achieve alone, but with the power of multiple investors, their capital can be aggregated to achieve it, providing investors with access.

For example, the iPartners platform was used to access a US-based venture capital secondaries fund. We aggregated approximately 75 investors, with amounts ranging from $50000 through to $2.5 million per investor, to invest a total of $45 million into the offshore fund, which had a minimum hurdle of $10 million to access the fund. This means 75 investors who historically had the door shut on them now have an access point to this institutional quality manager.

The growth in these access funds (sometimes called feeder funds because the capital flows through an Australian unit trust that 'feeds' into the offshore fund) in Australia has been unprecedented. Their estimated growth is more than $10 billion over the past few years, and I expect this to grow to more than $50 billion in the upcoming years as new investors allocate to alternative assets with improved access to educational content, existing investors allocate a larger percentage of their capital and the broad proliferation of iPartners-like platforms streamline the investment process.

Offshore single-asset exposure

If you don't want international exposure via an access fund run by fund managers, you can always go it alone and source single-asset exposure from overseas. However, I would be inclined to always partner and co-invest if I don't have any particular point of differentiation or expertise in the area. In private markets, more so than in public markets, local expertise is critical.

If you're going it alone, the first step would be to give yourself a quick course on currency. The movement on currency can be a gain or a loss for you when you translate your investment returns back to local currency.

For example, say you bought a $100000 loan denominated in USD paying you 10 per cent per annum, and the next day the AUD strengthened 10 per cent against the USD (which weakened). This currency move would wipe out your year's worth of coupon. If the AUD weakens 10 per cent against the USD, you've roughly doubled your expected return.

It's pretty much common sense. Just be careful when looking offshore that currency doesn't clean out all the benefits you were hoping to achieve, or add a level of risk you haven't considered.

On a global scale, alternatives are an enormous market, presenting significant choice. The currency of the investment as mentioned above is another risk to consider (some investors treat currency as an asset class in itself and actively look to take on the risk and trade them around, which for the skilled is a valid approach, but for most it's a great way to lose money), although it brings investors an opportunity to further diversify and add investments that may actually reduce their total risk on a portfolio basis. So an eye to global trends and opportunities is critical.

Hobbies, hedge funds and niche markets

Now that we've covered the main alternative asset classes you can invest in, let's discuss the rest. There's a random assortment of different alternative investment options (many of which I don't recommend investing in, aside from maybe a dabble for fun — but they're worth knowing about nonetheless).

Films and R&D

In Australia, providing capital to films or R&D (research and development) is potentially a tax-efficient way to invest due to offset benefits provided by the government to promote these alternative investment options, often reducing the risk of investing through a potential government-linked cash flow. This can make them attractive debt investments as long as they are structured the right way. Unless you get your documentation done well, any good investment can turn bad.

Even though the government rebates can reduce the risk of investing in these areas, it can be quite a bit of work to document and structure these investments, which has tended to make them less mainstream. However, with the right partner some interesting investing with quite an attractive risk-return profile can be done in R&D and films.

Intellectual property

This is a relatively new asset class and tends to reside with the specialist for the specific field that the intellectual property (IP) resides in. It includes elements such as film copyright, music, media, R&D (this is the sale, not financing R&D as above), brands, patents and patent portfolios.

All these items can in theory be unbundled, owned as stand-alone rights and held for pure accretion in value. They can have value purely as a scarce asset (that others may want to own, which hopefully generates value), or they can generate passive income production through royalties from the income produced from the IP. They can also be monetised through generating licensing fees from re-selling the right to utilise the IP, along with other benefits from owning the IP.

I don't come across these types of investment opportunities very often, although as they tend to be uncorrelated returns to other asset classes they can be interesting. The biggest challenge is bringing in the specialist knowledge to access the opportunity, as its unlikely a traditional investment manager or investors would have the skillset to access the opportunity. As such it likely remains a niche market.

Passion assets

Passion assets are things that people have a passion for owning or collecting. Think prestige cars, art, stamps, furniture, even patents. They are a genuine asset class, but I don't like them from an investor perspective because there are large commissions payable on entry and exit as well as being an insiders market. This makes the valuation of the assets very cloudy. For example, the commission on art can be as high as 20 or 30 per cent for both buying and selling. So you buy a painting for $1 million. If you sell that painting down the track for $1 million, you're only really getting $700 thousand ($1 million minus 30 per cent commission). You need that painting to go up to $1.4285 million ($1.4285 million minus 30 per cent commission) just to break even. From an economics perspective, it just doesn't strike me as a good trade.

I think the value of these assets is the pleasure side of it. Some people get personal enjoyment out of these collectibles. You can't really price this. So from an economic point of view, the potential value is limited. I'm sure the specialists in the field can make money, but for the rest of us, I suspect it will always be tough. Having said that, for those people who like to combine their passion with a little speculation, it can be a fun thing to do, so good on them!

Hedge funds

If you ask the average financial planner for recommendations for investing in alternatives, in addition to suggesting REITs, they will probably recommend loosely defined hedge funds. This advice can feel very outdated now. In Australia it's not uncommon to come across various hedge fund strategies in the equity space such as long-short or market neutral funds, but the majority of other hedge-fund-like strategies, particularly macro hedge funds, tend to be based in Asia or offshore. There are long-short equity hedge funds, macro hedge funds, merger or convertible arbitrage-type hedge funds, quantitative-based hedge funds (which use mathematical models to try and predict events), credit hedge funds, commodity hedge funds and all sorts of other hybrid strategies. If you want to get exposure to hedge funds in Australia, you're likely to only find them playing in listed equities.

Long-short hedge funds

To oversimplify: long-short hedge fund managers buy listed equities they think will go up, and they sell equities they think will go down. There are various ways of implementing these strategies.

'Long' is when you buy a share hoping it will rise in value. That's a pretty straightforward concept. 'Short' is a little trickier to get your head around in listed equities. It's when you sell a share that you have borrowed, hoping its value will fall before you have to give it back.

This is how short works: if you think some shares are going to fall, you borrow some of them from a prime broker (which tends to be associated with a bank), who's happy to lend you the equity if you pay them a fee. Then you sell those shares in the marketplace. When it comes time to give the borrowed shares back, you buy them back at the market price, which hopefully is lower than you sold them for. You then give them back to the lender. If your prediction is correct, the price has gone down and you make some money (because you sold them at a higher price than what you had to buy them back for).

For example, I *borrow* shares trading at $100 and I sell them at $100. Two weeks later that stock is trading at $90, so I buy it back at $90 and give it back to the person I borrowed it from. I sold at $100, bought at $90, and made $10, minus the borrow fee I would be charged.

A long-short manager will buy an equity today, if going long, for $100. After a month it's worth $110: they've just made $10 on their long. The same day they bought that equity for $100, they also borrowed shares to short a different equity, and they shorted that at $100. It gets to the end of the month and that equity is trading at $90, so they buy it back at $90, and they've made $10 on the short, as well as $10 on the long. They've made $20 (or more), again minus any borrowing costs (obviously both legs could have otherwise gone against them and they would have lost $20).

This strategy can be used on indexes, across sectors, within sectors — in fact, with all sorts of different things. You can even do it in different asset classes. Here I've explained how to do it in equities, but there are long-short funds in commodities and you can be long-short on rates or currencies. You can go short by selling futures (rather than the physical short explained above), and you can go short in a total return swap. You can do it effectively via an option strategy or you can physically short. Traditional long-short equity hedge funds will often sell a physical share to get the exact short position.

To do a long-short index trade, I might go long in the S&P 500 futures in the US market, and I might go short in the ASX 200 futures.

There are all sorts of different ways to play a long-short strategy. One is to be notionally matched, meaning you buy $100 in one share (long), and go short $100 in another. Or you might be volatility matched, meaning you buy an equity that has a volatility of 5 per cent, and you might put $100 into that, and you short an equity that has a volatility of, for example, 2.5 per cent, putting in $200. So in theory you have 5 per cent long volatility and 5 per cent short volatility but have different notional exposures on the long and short.

All these strategies are great when they work and the historical relationships hold true. They're less fun when they don't work — and history is not a good leading indicator of future moves!

Market neutral hedge funds

Another popular hedge fund strategy — a close cousin to long-short — is to be market neutral in nature, meaning in theory you don't care if the broader market goes up or down. You can do this within a sector long-short (e.g. in the energy sector) or you can be cross-sector (long energy, short retail). There are many variations of the style. And be aware that it never works perfectly in practice.

Market neutral basically means that you try to get to the point where you get market beta to neutral, or you're effectively zero. You are less sensitive if the market goes up or down, you should still make money and you're taking relative value plays rather than market plays.

The way fund managers try to be market neutral is they take bets on single stocks. As a simple example, if you have a $1 short BHP, a $1 long Rio Tinto and the market goes up by 50 per cent, you're taking limited market exposure when adjusted for the respective correlations. You've specifically got exposure to the movement of those shares, but you're market neutral in nature because the long in Rio Tinto and the short in BHP offset each other when you factor in expected correlation (the notional amounts will likely be slightly different from $1 in each due to the correlation effect). What could go wrong?

History would suggest quite a bit, although there are managers that outperform over time.

Hedge-fund replication

If an investor says to a bank or fund manager, 'I want to get access to a hedge fund, but I need liquidity', they might say, 'Well, I've got this hedge fund replication strategy. It tracks hedge-fund returns, but it's liquid.'

Hedge-fund replication is a quantitative method of attempting to replicate hedge-fund return using liquid market instruments such as derivatives, futures and liquid assets. It's trying to *replicate* a hedge-fund return profile (rather than owning the traditional hedge-fund assets) because hedge funds are illiquid.

Hedge funds typically trade in real things, such as equities, bonds and illiquid assets, whereas index replication attempts to use quantitative factors and various financial instruments to replicate the performance of a hedge fund (e.g. its return distribution and volatility). If a hedge fund was going long or short, instead of actually doing those trades, you'd try to replicate the performance of that by using any method your model tells you to. It sounds weird, but these mathematical models exist. If you have a mathematical model that says you can replicate the return on this hedge fund by using commodity futures, equity derivatives and interest rate swaps, it sounds totally ridiculous, but you basically combine factors and finance instruments to come up with a model designed to replicate the return of a hedge-fund strategy. That's index replication.

Historically, however, they have been pretty average at tracking hedge-fund returns. The models don't hang together for long periods of time. I don't like them and would never invest in them. The banks are notorious for marketing overly fitted quant-based indexes (which are indexes that are created by mathematicians looking at lots of historic asset price movements and then creating an investment strategy that would have worked perfectly if implemented historically, and assuming it will work perfectly moving forward).

Litigation funding

Let's say a company that does litigation has 10 cases for clients that they think are going to win, although they (or their clients) don't currently have the funds to cover all their legal costs. You can effectively fund these cases through lending money to cover the cost of the litigation and you typically get paid a fixed-income-like return and potential upside. If they win some or all of the cases, they likely get some potential windfall. If they lose too many of them, you can obviously lose money. There are litigation funds where you can put money into a fund that is used just to fund litigation on an ongoing basis. This investment can be considered a bit like other asset-backed investments (the expected payout is a bit like a receivable, as explained in earlier chapters) that we have discussed, with litigation outcomes being the security. Historically it has been an okay investment and structured the right way has some merit for investors.

Insurance-linked products

Investing in insurance exposures is an alternative asset that gives investors the opportunity to get insurance-company-like returns without being an insurance company. The insurance-linked market is very institutional. Insurance companies play in this space to sell some of their risk to third parties as a risk-management approach, and institutional credit managers do too, but it's typically not a direct investor alternative as it's hard to access. Still, it's worth mentioning as it has the potential to become more mainstream through investment platforms such as iPartners.

Insurance-linked investments can be seen as worthwhile because insurance has low correlation to other asset classes. Insurance events are random and unpredictable, so you might get a positive payout while equities are falling, for example. In practice they are a bit like structured notes in that they tend to combine a cash position (debt obligation) with a real insurance position, often embedded through a derivative contract. You typically get paid a high fixed-income-like return in exchange for running the risk of losing some or all of your capital if the pre-specified insured event occurs.

There are two key insurance products: longevity notes and catastrophe notes.

Longevity notes

With longevity notes, you get paid for taking on some of the risks that insurance companies take on. You can take on a certain cohort, investing in whether they're going to live for a long time or for a shorter period of time. It relates to longevity — how long people live for — because that's a genuine risk insurers run. For example, if the insurer is paying out on a lifetime annuity (basically a lifetime fixed-income product), the longer people live, the longer the insurer needs to pay out on that annuity product. If insurers wanted to reduce some of the risk that people live longer than forecast, one way to do it would be via offering a longevity-linked structured note, which is really the combination of a longevity swap (just think of it as a contract transferring the risk of the life insurer to the investor — a bit like a derivative contract) plus a debt instrument such as a term deposit.

The investor will receive a nice regular coupon, although if the pool of underlying annuity receivers (for example) live longer than the modelled forecast, the insurer will pay out more than they expected, which may reduce the investor's coupon (as the insurer transferred this risk to the investor through the longevity swap) and the investor may also lose some of their coupons and/or principal. It's a bit morbid, but if people live longer than the insurer's model forecasts the longevity note holder will lose money!

Catastrophe notes

Catastrophe notes are structurally a similar concept, but for disaster insurance rather than life insurance related risk. To lessen some of their risk, insurance companies offer and sell disaster-linked structured notes.

For example, you invest $100 into an asset, and across five years it pays you 10 per cent per annum, and you will get your money back as long as (for example) there are no tornados in a certain region of the United States that wipe out an entire suburb that the insurance company has to pay out on. It's really providing sub-underwriting to insurance companies through insurance notes.

Catastrophe notes are risky, but how risky they are depends on how they're structured. For example, if the insurance company says, 'If there's a tornado in this region of the United States, at the first dollar of a loss you need to pay out a certain amount of money', your risk is higher. Alternatively, they could say, 'In the event that the loss is greater than $10 million, you need to make a payout.' It depends on how the contract is structured. Buying these investments is effectively taking on some of the risk that insurance companies take on, to generate an investment return.

Historically, the payment on these exposures has actually been quite good for investors. It's been a reasonably attractive asset class to invest in. It can perform well for a long period of time because it tends to be a really low probability event — but if it does occur the loss can be quite significant.

Volatility

Volatility is another asset class you can invest in. It can be used as a low correlation exposure to add to a portfolio, as a hedge for other asset classes to protect the portfolio or as a stand-alone to generate returns.

There is a VIX index (Chicago Board Options Exchange's CBOE Volatility Index) in the United States, which is quite popular, where you can simply buy volatility (as in, buy VIX Futures). It's a pretty cool asset to have if markets crash. Volatility has a low correlation and often negative correlation to equity markets, which means it tends to go up when equity markets fall, and it tends to go down when equity markets go up.

If you are wanting to protect your portfolio, a nice way to do it would be to have a position in long volatility. If the equity market falls, you'd of course lose money on your equity portfolio, but you'd likely make some money on your long volatility position; they're offsetting to a degree, making them hedge like. It is not a free lunch though. If volatility does nothing or falls, you'll lose money on the long volatility position, but as an investor it may be okay to have the hedge position in place as a risk-reducing overlay.

To complicate things, there are other ways to trade volatility. These are called option straddles/strangles. You try to end up with a position where you're removing the sensitivity to market moves (delta) from a derivative position. Once you take the price move out of your position you are left with closer to a pure volatility position. So if you want to be 'long vol' or 'short vol', you can use derivatives to create those positions. The main takeaway is that you can create a long volatility position through a derivatives strategy, which may benefit you as an investor if volatility goes up (often when markets crash), or a short volatility position, which should benefit you if volatility goes down.

Another approach used by institutional types is to buy variance swaps across a certain maturity. This can also be an interesting position. In a simple sense, variance is volatility squared.

How do you invest in volatility?

For most of us, the easiest way would be to simply invest in an ETF (exchange traded fund) that tracks the VIX index or into a fund with a similar strategy. The VIX index is quite easy to access for the average investor. More institutional investors might try to be more sensitive on how they trade their position, so they're more likely to directly use a derivative position, whether in options or variance. And there are hedge funds that trade purely in volatility. But the average investor will simply buy via a fund or index ETF and an institutional investor will usually do it via a derivative strategy.

Note: Inexperienced investors should be wary of investing in volatility-linked ETFs as the accumulated losses from owning may never be recouped, even in a market sell off. In a normal market the ETF is typically losing money, so you could lose a lot before you potentially benefit from a spike in the ETF value driven by a market crash.

Crypto assets

I have been watching crypto's evolution from the side lines. I see very broad application for the underlying technology, in particular combining some of the older school financial engineering with smart contract/blockchain-like solutions. Blockchain is the technology that securely records, stores and tracks transactions automatically, and smart contracts are automated contracts between buyers and sellers.

Crypto currencies can be purchased, sold and loaned on various exchanges. The two best-known forms are Bitcoin and Ether, but there are many more. Crypto is also gaining traction as a currency for buying goods and services.

A number of ETFs (exchange traded funds) are appearing, although I'm not yet convinced that it makes sense to take a passive set-and-forget exposure to crypto currencies evidenced by the significant price falls. As an investor you'd want to be very comfortable with volatility through the mark-to-market on your position and the longer term prospects of the respective crypto currencies. For most I suspect you'd be better off investing through a crypto fund with a more dynamic asset allocation approach.

If I were interested in the crypto space, I'd be considering asset allocation through crypto trading funds. My observation is that traders implementing currency/option/volatility-based trading-like strategies, along with high frequency trading models, are generating attractive returns from a largely uninformed and unregulated marketplace.

In this situation I would much prefer to outsource to a specialist with the time and resources to trade the market. But that said, at the time of writing, this is a highly volatile, fraud-riddled, largely speculative asset class to invest in that I am largely avoiding.

Conclusion

If you're just starting out in investing, odds are you've gone to a financial planner and been offered the routine, off-the-shelf investment portfolio, which typically won't include alternative assets of much interest, because alternatives aren't off the shelf. Or maybe you trade the stock market yourself, but haven't yet accessed the true diversity and new world of low correlation investing in your portfolio. Even if you are a seasoned investor, you might not be getting the best returns for each dollar if you haven't got alternatives in your portfolio. Sure, it takes more time and research to invest in alternatives, but it's well worth it and hopefully this book speeds up your understanding of this asset class.

It's about being smart and knowing where to look. Wherever there's a scarcity of capital or knowledge, there's an opportunity. Structure your trades to make sure you align your interests with other investors and capital raisers to ensure optimal outcomes. Do this by embedding incentives in your terms — making sure their money is on the line before yours if it goes pear-shaped. This combination of scarcity of capital and alignment of interests is the sweet spot for a better risk-return ratio.

There are many different types of alternative assets, but the biggest, and probably the easiest to understand if you are a newbie, is property. There's a lot of property development that the banks won't touch because the LVR doesn't suit their modelling. Banks are not as adventurous or creative as they used to be, and this is where non-bank lenders such as iPartners can come in and offer investments at a higher interest rate. They might refinance with the bank after the loan matures, but in the meantime you've earned a tidy sum of interest for 12 or 18 months. It's a win-win.

Investing in equity is a bit more complex to get right for newcomers because you need to do serious due diligence on the company no matter the stages of investment (angel to growth), and you need to choose a method: from straight equity to deferred or preferred, to convertible notes and SAFE notes. You might find you need to go back over chapter 5 (equity) when opportunities arise, to make sure you understand all the variables.

If this more complicated financial world of investing is new to you, you also might find yourself going back to chapter 6 (credit) to review all the different levels and types of credit more than once. I've done my best to set them out in simple language, but credit's no simple thing! So feel free to dip back in when you need to — that's what this book is for. It's a resource so you can educate yourself and make more informed decisions, rather than missing out entirely on the opportunities in alternative assets.

When we started iPartners, our aim was to open up the alternative assets market to individual investors. Investors like you and me. Why should it just be the playground of large institutions and super-rich families? Now, thanks to the power of aggregated investments through platforms such as ours, more and more people can play in the space and take greater control over growing their personal wealth.

To dig further into potential investment opportunities, please register at:

iPartners.com.au/register